377
AF654418

Gandhian Philosophy of Voluntarism

About the Author

Dr. A. K. Sharma is P. K. Kelkar Chair Professor of Sociology, Indian Institute of Technology Kanpur. Dr. Sharma has had extensive experience in analysis and evaluation of development programmes in the country, and is working with professionals and non-governmental organizations. He has published extensively in national and international journals. A winner of the Chandrasekaran Award, Dr. Sharma has authored six books including *Gattdhian Perspective on Population and Development*. His areas of interest include evaluation of rural development programmes, health sociology, and Gandhian theory. Dr. Sharma has provided consultancy in about 37 research and consultancy projects sponsored by national and international agencies like GTZ, Population Council, Pathfinders International, MEADOW, UNICEF. NACO, JSK, BSNL, CSIR, ICSSR. Ministry of Rural Development (Government of India), Government of Uttar Pradesh, Ministry of Tribal Affairs, and NGOs like Banwasi Seva Asharam.

Gandhian Philosophy of Voluntarism

A Comparative Study of Development in the Ashram Villages and Outside

A. K. Sharma
Humanities and Social Sciences Department
IIT Kanpur

CONCEPT PUBLISHING COMPANY PVT. LTD.
NEW DELHI-110059

© A.K. Sharma

All rights reserved. No part of this work may be reproduced, stored, adapted, or transmitted in any form or by any means, electronic, mechanical, photocopying, micro-filming recording or otherwise, or translated in any language, without the prior written permission of the copyright owner and the publisher. The book is sold subject to the condition that it shall not, by way of trade or otherwise, be lent, resold, hired out, or otherwise circulated without the prior publisher's written consent in any form of binding or cover other than that in which it is published.

The views and opinions expressed in this book are author(s) own and the facts reported by them/her have been verified to the extent possible, and the publishers are not in any way liable for the same.

ISBN-13 : 978-93-5125-076-0

First Published 2014

Published and Printed by

Concept
Since 1974

Concept Publishing Company Pvt. Ltd.
A/15-16, Commercial Block, Mohan Garden
New Delhi-110059 (India)
T: 25351460, 25351794, *F*: 091-11-25357109
E: publishing@conceptpub.com, W: www.conceptpub.com
Editorial Office: H-13, Bali Nagar, New Delhi-110 015, India.

Cataloging in Publication Data—*Courtesy:* D.K. Agencies (P) Ltd. <docinfo@dkagencies.com>

Sharma, A. K., 1953-
Gandhian philosophy of voluntarism : a comparative study of development in the Ashram villages and outside / A.K. Sharma.
p. cm.
Includes bibliographical references (p.) and index.
ISBN 9789351250760

1. Banwasi Seva Ashram. Mahatma Gandhi Mission. 2. Rural development projects--India—Sonbhadra (District) 3. Voluntarism—India—Sonbhadra (District) I. Title.

DDC 307.141209542 23

Dedicated

to

(Late) Dr Clymes Augustine

Preface

This book is based on the study of the Banwasi Seva Ashram, which has been working for sixty years in tribal areas of district Sonbhadra, U.P. The draft report on the Banwasi Seva Ashram (BSA) was submitted in August 2012 by Ms. Rita Singh on behalf of the WIZMIN Management Consultants, Kanpur. Dr. Ragini Prem, Secretary of the BSA circulated it among activists and intellectuals. We have received detailed comments from some of them including Dr. Prem herself. Several of them which require explanation of figures or are of factual nature have been incorporated in the revised report without affecting the findings, conclusion or objectivity of the report. Yet, there are some perspectival issues which need to be dealt separately. Therefore, a separate Epilogue has been added to the report. The WIZMIN team discussed some comments and made changes while finalizing the earlier draft itself. For further changes and Epilogue, however, only the author is responsible.

IIT Kanpur
July 2013

A.K. Sharma

Acknowledgements

I am thankful to Banwasi Seva Ashram for giving me the opportunity to carry out this evaluation. This was a task of huge responsibility, and when we started the work, we were aware of the challenges ahead. Without the support and cooperation of several people, it would not have been possible to accomplish this task.

I am grateful to Dr. Ragini Prem for the time she gave us. Her vivid narration of events and passion made it easier for researchers to capture the essence of five decades of works of the Ashram. I and the researchers associated with WIZMIN had several rounds of interesting discussions with her and Shubhaji, during which we could freely give critique of their work. Frank exchange of ideas was only possible because both of them were always open for new ideas and were ready to seek objective feedback on Ashram's work.

I am thankful to the staff of Banwasi Seva Ashram for providing all the information we asked for. They never refused our demand for data even if it meant digging out old files or sifting through reams of pages. The lengthy discussions we had with Vimal Bhai, Shiv Sharan Bhai, Lal Bahadur Bhai, Ravi Chandra Dubey Bhai and Naresh Yadav Bhai, made working on this report interesting.

The study was done under the leadership of Ms. Rita Singh, who not only inspired and guided the research, but who also patiently went through the report several times. I am grateful to her for shaping this report and helping me develop future course of action for the Ashram. I am also indebted to Dr. Ragni Prem, Dr. G.D. Agarwal, Mr. Dunu Roy and Mrs. Anna-Maria De Witte for their comments on the original report.

At the end, I thank all those villagers and volunteers who so willingly accepted us and responded to us. Their feedback formed the core of the report, and we are truly indebted to them. The spirit of staff of the Ashram and people of Sonbhadra got rubbed on each one of us, and we all took several extra steps to make this report useful to them. I wish them success and happiness.

A.K. Sharma
IIT Kanpur

Contents

List of Tables

List of Figures

List of Boxes

List of Photos

List of Map

The Survey Team

Rita Singh	Project Leader
Dr. A.K. Sharma	Expert, Professor of Sociology, Dept of HSS, IIT Kanpur
Naresh Mishra	Supervisor
R.R. Senger	Supervisor
Rajesh Sharma	Investigator
Ranjita Singh	Investigator
Shaily Agnihotri	Analyst
Nirmala Devi	Investigator
Shikha Sinha	Investigator
Smita Singh	Investigator
Zahid Khan	Investigator
Sudhir Tiwari	Investigator
Gayatri Singh	Analyst
Umesh Dixit	Data Processing
Dharampal Singh	Data Entry Operator
Vivek Kumar	Data Entry Operator

CHAPTER 1

Introduction

The strategy should be (1) to use the local resources available with the people and the community in the first instance, to employ idle or wasted labour for the development of wasted land-water-plants and animal resources in an integrated and balanced fashion to promote healthy environment, to change and propagate social values for the use of technology information, equipments, production-system and goods, (2) to demonstrate to the people and the governments models of sustainable development, viable and self-generative patterns of agriculture, forestry, animal husbandry, pollution free-village industries, inexpensive community based health and medical services, (3) to press the government and bank officials and resources into service of the people, to make the people aware of their potentials and entitlements, to educate the people and organize them to secure their social, legal and economic entitlements, to specially press for the time bound implementation of the anti-poverty plans and the minimum needs programme of the government and the banks, (4) to use the donors' money to fill in the gaps, to experiment and find new paths, to demonstrate viable and sustainable models of development, for training of community leaders and youths, to implement programmes for which local resources are not available and to provide for the flexibility starting capital and margin money to mobilise indigenous resources, on an accelerated pace.

(Prem Bhai)

This book presents the findings of the evaluation study of the Banwasi Seva Ashram's Agrindus project running in the predominantly tribal areas of district Sonbhadra (UP). The study was commissioned in year 2011 by the donors to WIZMIN, Kanpur through the Banwasi Seva Ashram, under technical supervision of Dr. A.K. Sharma, Professor of Sociology in Indian Institute of Technology Kanpur. This chapter presents a brief history of the Banwasi Seva Ashram and the Agrindus project, earlier evaluations of the project and purpose, conceptual framework and objectives of this study.

1.1 The Banwasi Seva Ashram

The Banwasi Seva Ashram in Uttar Pradesh was set up in 1954. It is one of the most known of the Gandhian voluntary organizations operating in different parts of the country—like Odisha, Assam, Bihar, Bengal, Uttarakhand and Madhya Pradesh. Located in southern part of Sonbhadra district of Uttar Pradesh, the Ashram has been working for last five decades to bring about integrated development in the tribal villages. The Ashram activities are based on Gandhian principles of Swaraj (i.e. development through self-rule) and Sarvodaya (i.e. development of all). According to the Ashram, one of the aims of the Ashram was to present an example of development to be brought about through the efforts of a dedicated leadership, envisioning of plans for a holistic development, and attempts to produce results. For this the Ashram relied on the approach which, in modern parlance, may be called the participatory or inclusionary approach. This has produced changes in the lives of people both in terms of economic development and thinking. The Ashram started its activities, under the leadership of Shri Prem Bhai, a noted Gandhian activist, at a time when the region lacked infrastructure, drinking water, health and education facilities. The region also lacked any interaction with the outside world. The only thing the people of this region exchanged from outside was salt. During more than five decades of its existence, the Banwasi Seva Ashram has engaged in diversified areas, with the goal of transforming the isolated rural society of Sonbhadra district.

The stated objectives of the Ashram are as follows: (http://home.iitk.ac.in/~avrs/NGOWebsite/Mission1.htm):

1. Empowerment of the people through socio-economic and educational activities in order to develop holistically under privileged village communities.
2. Development of a self-sufficient, harmonious society by encouraging people to live according to the principles of Sarvodaya (development of all) and Gram Swarajya (self-reliance).
3. Capacity building of the Ashram staff and village functionaries in order to guarantee the success of the development process.
4. Support youth volunteers from all over India to work in the direction of Gram Swarajya (self-reliance).

Keeping in view the above objectives the Ashram has been quite active on various fronts for almost sixty years and many things have been achieved. However, the milieu has completely changed now. Today, villages have access to new facilities and new ideas. Industries have moved into the area with power plants, dams and large manufacturing units. This also means that villagers are exposed to new risks such as climate change, air and water pollution, fall in forest and agricultural produce, unemployment, increasing unrest, and alienation. One cannot ignore the fact that the Ashram's development activities are occurring in the villages which belong to a state and a nation. Thus there is a significant confounding effect of the changes in the wider socio-political structures on the final outcome of the Ashram activities. In this context, one requires a holistic study of the outcome of the Ashram's development activities without ignoring the role of media, perceived economic opportunities brought about by globalization, changes taking place in the value system among youths and socio-political impact of government's policies and activities.

It is claimed (in a personal interview with the Secretary) that at present the Ashram is primarily involved in the following activities:

1. Building up people's resistance specially of villagers against increasing environmental pollution;

2. Empowering people to derive maximum benefits from the government development schemes and assertion in Panchayati Raj Institution (PRI);
3. Creating pressure for proper implementation of Forest Rights Act, 2006.
4. Empowerment of women by involving them in family and community development; and
5. Social and life orientation of the adolescents and the young people.

1.2 A Brief History of the Agrindus Project

The Agrindus Institute was set up in 1967-68 to boost the agro-industrial development of the area. For this, the Ashram was supported by the UP Gandhi Smarak Nidhi (Gandhi Memorial Fund), the Sarva Seva Sangh, Path Finder Fund and the British NGO, War on Want. This was the time when Mr. Prem Bhai entered the Ashram area. The aim of the institute was to boost the agricultural and industrial development of the area and take up relief operations during draughts and other natural disasters. In 1956-58 the Ashram got 250 acres of land from the state government and planned to build an ideal, self-reliant village on that. The plan included demonstration, training through work, and extension activities. To quote:

> The goal has been to create a sense of self-reliance in communities by establishing village funds, making individuals and communities accept responsibility for paying for services and reimbursing all assistance received for the creation of capital assets. Individuals and families are also encouraged to be fully autonomous so they can implement all the schemes and activities included in the programme.
> The 250 acres of land received from government was hilly and unproductive scrubland. The first task was to turn this into a demonstration farm, using an integrated watershed development plan. This included landscaping, harvesting of rainwater, improved agricultural techniques, agro-forestry as well as elements of town planning. (Hoddy, 1999)

In her works on the Agrindus Institute, Elizabeth Hoddy (1999) used the term Agrindus Institute interchangeably with the Banwasi Seva Ashram. Thus the evaluation of Agrindus Institute is the assessment of the impact of the Banwasi Seva Ashram. To an outsider it is difficult to distinguish between the activities of the Ashram from those of the Agrindus Institute. This study also follows the same tradition. Yet, one can see that there is a trend. Initially, the Ashram concentrated on the implementation of schemes of agricultural and industrial development, and gradually it diversified to other fields such as health and education as the other needs of the rural poor were also to be attended to. In the 70's brick kilns, promotion of khadi and village industries, accepting responsibility for harvesting minor forest produce were introduced. Pathfinder fund had supported the family welfare project which was for the promotion of small, planned family through health care extension programme.

Elizabeth Hoddy (1999) divides the history of Agrindus Institute into five phases. *The first phase* (1967-73) was devoted to land development and irrigation. *The second phase* (1974-80) was devoted to the concept of Whole Village Development with the four basic thrusts: (1) mobilization of people for community development; (2) initiation of a process of sharing resources and means of production; (3) training of community leaders and village technicians to undertake this kind of development; (4) organization of services and technical guidance necessary for integrated community development. In 1974 the Ashram conducted a survey of 105 villages with financial support from the government which was to understand the problems of rural people and develop appropriate schemes for them. *The third phase* (1981-85) focused on extension work and experimentation. During this phase efforts were made to mobilize funds from all sources: government, large industrial companies, bank loans and tapping of international non-government funding agencies. In 1975 the Banwasi Seva Ashram received donation from two German NGOs, the Protestant Central Agency (EZE) and Bread for the World (BFW) for Village Development Plan of 100 villages after the survey of 105 villages with the help of the government funds. Under Mahatma Gandhi Mission, among other things, a fund was set up (by EZE, later called

EED, and BFW) to promote similar voluntary action in other areas and a Small Project Fund (SPF) was set up to benefit the rural poor and other regions through voluntary efforts of the local youth. Some major attainments of this phase are opening of ration shops, putting pressure on government teachers by appointing own teachers in the villages, and putting a Public Interest Litigation (PIL) in the Supreme Court for freedom of bonded labour and for land rights (Banwasi Seva Ashram, 2006) in favour of traditional forest dwellers who were threatened by the forest department under the pretext that the land was proposed for reserved forest. *The fourth phase* (1986-1990) saw the continuation and consolidation of the activities initiated during the third phase and special efforts were made to settle land disputes, create awareness about women's position, spread education, and promote self-reliance in health care. This was also the time when the Government of India included villages under Integrated Rural Development Programme (IRDP), combining several of the previously implemented rural development schemes. Evaluation of IRDP at the national level has brought out many faults in the implementation of IRDP and the Ashram attempted to ensure that IRDP is implemented effectively and through people's participation involving its own three-tier village organization. *The fifth phase* (1990-96) focused on Total Literacy Campaign (TLC). In addition, the Ashram has implemented various rural development schemes launched by the Central Government and also its own schemes without compromising with the Gandhian philosophy of Swadeshi and Swavlamban.

1.3 Previous Evaluations

There have been several attempts in the past to study and evaluate the activities of the Ashram or the activities under Agrindus Institute/ programme, formally and informally. Many scholars and organizations from India and abroad have been associated with the works of the Ashram. Notable among them are Dr. K.K. Mukherjee of Delhi University's Department of Social Work, Mr. P. Rajadurai, a veteran development consultant, the Magsaysay Award winner Mr. L.C. Jain, an ex-Vice-Chancellor of Pune University, Mr. Devadatt Dabholkar, noted environmentalist Prof. G.D.

Agarwal, and the American scholar Dr. Paul Clements. Some of the studies were done by outsiders and some by the Ashram functionaries and the people. Yet, they pertained mostly to some specific programme or activity launched by the Ashram. Elizabeth Hoddy's *The Banwasi Seva Ashram*, written under the guidance of Mr. L.C. Jain and published in 1999 by Gandhi Peace Foundation, is one of the most comprehensive works on the Ashram activities from its inception to 1996. The Total Literacy Campaign (TLC) was evaluated by an external team, under the leadership of Mr. Devadatt Dabholkar, ex-Vice Chancellor of Pune University, who concluded that the TLC had made a significant contribution to educational status of people in the project area. In 2006 Ramagundam Rahul's *Social Warrior: Nurturing Village based Constructive Workers for Gram Swarajya*, was published from Banwasi Seva Ashram Mahatma Gandhi Mission. In 2005-06 Dr. A.K. Sharma from Indian Institute of Technology, Kanpur and Dr. Clymes Augustine from Christ Church College, Kanpur conducted fieldwork in a few project blocks of the Ashram and submitted their report to the Ashram.

In year 2002 an independent evaluation of the works of the Agrindus was done by Smt. Uma Ramaswami and Smt. Hemlata. They were sent by the donors to evaluate the Integrated Rural Development Programmes (IRDP). In their report they praised the works done by the Ashram in diverse fields, particularly in the field of land rights. They specifically mentioned achievements in water conservation, social forestry, irrigation, agricultural development, horticulture, khadi and village industry and "life education". In the same year the educational activities of the Ashram were evaluated by National Council of Educational Research and Training (NCERT) and the US agency, Christian Children Fund (CCF). Around the same time the international NGO, Aide et Action, developed guidelines for evaluation of educational schemes of the Ashram. They suggested that the evaluation should include understanding of activists and beneficiaries regarding the goals, strategies and policies, scope and limitations of the present education system, linkages with other similar NGOs, and socially relevant and stable educational possibilities (Banwasi Seva Asharm, 2003).

1.4 Purpose of the Study

The above works on the Ashram activities have shown that from the beginning Ashram had adopted a problem solving and participatory approach rather than a delivery approach. This helped greatly in building trust among people and enabling them to solve problems arising out of tribal, caste and class conflicts, and also the problems caused by social change. This has also empowered people in the Ashram area to think about themselves, society and environment. It was expected that this trust and empowerment would facilitate rural development works undertaken by the government also in different sectors. However, there have been some critical reflections on the Ashram activities among the critics and intellectuals associated with the Ashram. While continuing to admire the Gandhian philosophy of voluntarism followed by the Ashram, talking specifically in the context of responses to the problem of environmental pollution, Prof. G.D. Agarwal expressed a bit of unhappiness over the fact that as time passed, in certain domains the Ashram activities showed a shift from Gandhian philosophy to a socialist philosophy of development, i.e. a shift from participatory and self-reliant approach to delivery and survival approach.

The purpose of this study is explore the overall impact of the Ashram activities on development and psychology of people and through that on implementation of government schemes launched under the aegis of rural development. The later activities include Mahatma Gandhi National Rural Employment Guarantee Act (MNREGA), Indira Awas Yojana (IAY), social security schemes for the old, widows, and physically challenged, Total Sanitation Campaign (TSC), and much talked about Right to Education. However, there will be special reference to activities launched under Agrindus' concept.

1.5 Objectives and Research Questions

The main objective of this study is to examine the processes of development in the Ashram villages and outside and their consequences for holistic and sustainable development of the people. This study will also examine the major strengths and weaknesses of major approaches to development and suggest an appropriate model of development suited to rural context, especially in the context where there is a large concentration of tribal population. This attempts to answer the following research questions:

1. Does ideology mediate the impact of interventions on the well-being of the people? Specifically, do the ideas of Swaraj and Sarvodaya lead to a sense of well-being among the people?
2. In the light of recent development efforts made by the state, does the Ashram need to reformulate its strategies or change some of its priorities? Where should they focus more?
3. How can the state and NGOs work synergistically in the interest of people's development?
4. What have been the priorities in development in villages under Asharm activities and other villages?
5. What is the difference in objective and subjective measures of well-being between Ashram villages and other villages?
6. Do the youth and elderly people in Ashram villages and other villages differ in terms of measures of well-being?
7. What are the differences in approaches to sustainability of assets created under Agrindus Institute and other development programmes between the Ashram villages and other villages?
8. Are the Ashram villages doing better than other villages in implementation of rural development schemes started by Government of India?
9. What are the organizational and institutional differences in development planning between the Ashram villages and the other villages?
10. Does the local administration follow a different approach to development in the Ashram villages and the other villages?

1.6 Conceptual Scheme

Before commissioning this study, Dr. Ragini Prem, Secretary of the Ashram had discussed the possibility of conducting an independent study of impact of their works in the project villages over the past decades. She wanted to get feedback from independent consultants about the strengths and weaknesses of their approaches and the impact of all development programmes. At that time she had all the Ashram activities in mind including the Agrindus concept. However, since this study is sponsored by the donors of the Agrindus Institute the activities pursued by the Institute had to become the major focus of the study. Moreover, a conceptual problem had to arise in evaluation of the activities of the Agrindus Institute. Here the issue was: What are the definitions and aims of development? The Ashram, the development experts and the people define development in different ways. Fieldwork done by A.K. Sharma and Clymes Augustine had already identified some of these complexities.

Keeping the complexity of issues and subjective-objective dimension of development in mind, we decided to use structured interview schedule to identify major project activities, their short term and long term impact, and the contribution to well- being measures. Comparison between control and experimental areas was taken for evaluation of projects. Qualitative research methods were used to explore people's meaning systems and how they define project contributions.

Discussing with the Ashram functionaries, development experts and the native people, a conceptual framework of development was developed. Figure 1.1 presents this framework. The conceptual

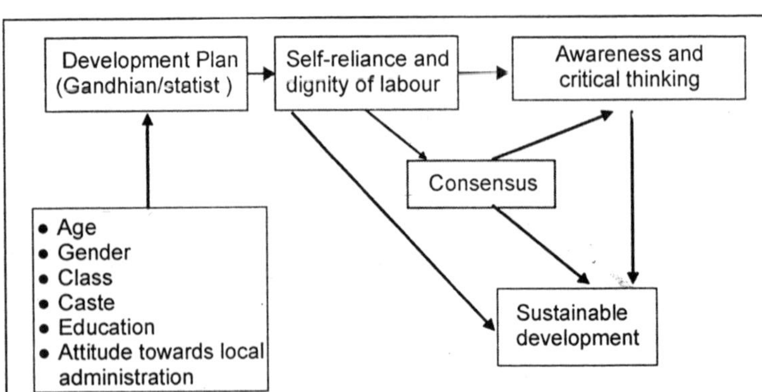

Fig. 1.1: Proposed model for impact of development plan on sustainable development

framework assumes that the aim of rural development is sustainable development. This requires a desire for self-reliance and dignity of labour, awareness and critical thinking and consensus on major issues. All of them depend heavily on the model of development planning which could be Gandhian or statist. Finally, the planning model does not come from nowhere. It is an outcome of social structure, social capital and education.

1.7 Organization of the Report

The book is divided into ten chapters. Following the present chapter, Chapter 2 is devoted to methodology. Chapter 3 focuses on institution building. Chapters 4-7 present the findings of the analysis on substantive issues: education, agriculture, village industries and health. Chapter 8 is focused on social issues addressed by the Ashram. Chapter 9 presents the summary of findings and attempts to answer questions raised above. This also includes some discussion of the limitations of the Agrindus Institute. Chapter 10 is on recommendations regarding what the Banwasi Seva Ashram can do in the future.

CHAPTER 2

Methodology

Evaluating works of organizations like the Banwasi Seva Ashram or of the projects like the Agrindus Institute is challenging because they involve both new ideas and services, not in one chosen area of activity but in different areas (conceivably in all areas of human activities). The first and foremost question is: Is one to evaluate the performance of the Ashram in developing the project area, or cost-effectiveness of strategies used, or the achievements of the project, or the change in the mind set of the people, or everything. Looked at from the perspective of project evaluation the usual course to be followed in the evaluation study is to relate various financial and other costs of the project to quantified indices of various tangible and non-tangible results—some intended, some unintended. Yet, the Agrindus Institute was to go beyond the issue of productivity and employment and was an attempt to change the definition of development. Thus it begs the question, "What is development?" Answer to this question is related to another question, "Development for whom?" Development experts realize that a holistic development has to be embedded in the socio-cultural beliefs and values of people. Besides being sensitive to the indigenous or local patterns of earning livelihood by people it also has to take care of sustainability of its approach and the empowerment of people who feel the brunt of isolation, poverty and rigid social stratification.

Social scientists have repeatedly pointed out that mere economic and state based models of development have not brought much fruition for several reasons:

(a) At the grassroots level there is lack of consensus regarding policies;
(b) People are not sufficiently aware of programmes and policies initiated by government;
(c) Government efforts are inadequate and marred by bureaucracy, inefficiency and corruption;
(d) Approaches to development lack a participatory approach;
(e) There is not enough emphasis on integration and moral questions; and
(f) They do not address the special needs of the marginalized and alienated sections of society.

This study enjoys a mixed method approach. A survey was conducted to assess the socio-economic conditions in the Ashram and other villages, and study beliefs, attitudes, and experiences of development in the two areas. This included use of well designed pre-tested and comprehensive questionnaires covering all aspects of rural development. These questionnaires were administered separately to youths, adults, village heads, faith healers and school teachers. Quantitative data are collected by properly trained investigators, and qualitative exercises are collected by senior experts. SPSS package was used for analysis of quantitative data. From the list of the project and non-project villages a representative sample of villages (to be used as intervention and control villages) was taken using probability method. It was also thought that for most purposes a sample of size 500-1000 would be enough to provide estimates with small (less than 5% error) in any particular category. This would also take care of the design effect.

The findings of the survey are supplemented by qualitative and participatory approaches such as interviews and focus group discussion (FGD). The key respondents for interviews are drawn from formal and informal elite, block and district level administrators, functionaries of the Ashram and beneficiaries of the different schemes. FGDs are conducted separately among men and women, adults and young people, tribal and non-tribal communities. The qualitative data produced useful insights into the psychological, institutional and spiritual aspects of development.

2.1 Sample Design

Using a multistage sampling method, respondents were reached sequentially through selection of six blocks, 40 villages and about 20 respondents from each village. A three stage sample selection process was used.

In the ***first stage*** blocks were selected — all four of the blocks where the Ashram has been active, namely Babhni, Chopan, Dudhi and Myorepur, were chosen for the study. To avoid the effect of diffusion, i.e. to avoid the effect of spread of ideas and practices from the Ashram blocks to other neighbouring blocks, two blocks from the northern part of the district were to be chosen for comparison. In the northern part there is no work of the Ashram and much of the northern part is Naxalite infected. This was clear from the beginning that the Ashram blocks may differ from the northern blocks in terms of composition of population, infrastructure and development activities. It was also in mind that this comparison may also shed some light on whether the activities of the Ashram have contributed to peace. Out of the four non-Ashram blocks of the district, Ghorawal and Nagwa blocks were selected.

In the ***second stage*** village selection was carried out in the following steps:

1. List of villages where Ashram carried out intensive programmes, i.e. where almost all programmes were launched, was taken. From these villages using simple random sampling (SRS) method 20 villages were selected.
2. A list of those villages was also taken where the Ashram largely conducted awareness programmes. From this list 10 villages were selected using SRS method.
3. From the non-Ashram villages, using SRS 5 villages were selected from Ghorawal and Nagwa blocks each. Map 2.1 shows the location of the survey villages.

Table 2.1 shows the list of all the villages selected for the survey.

In each village a list of all members of all households was made. A total of 5,720 households were listed and information was collected from 28,210 individuals spread across 6 blocks and

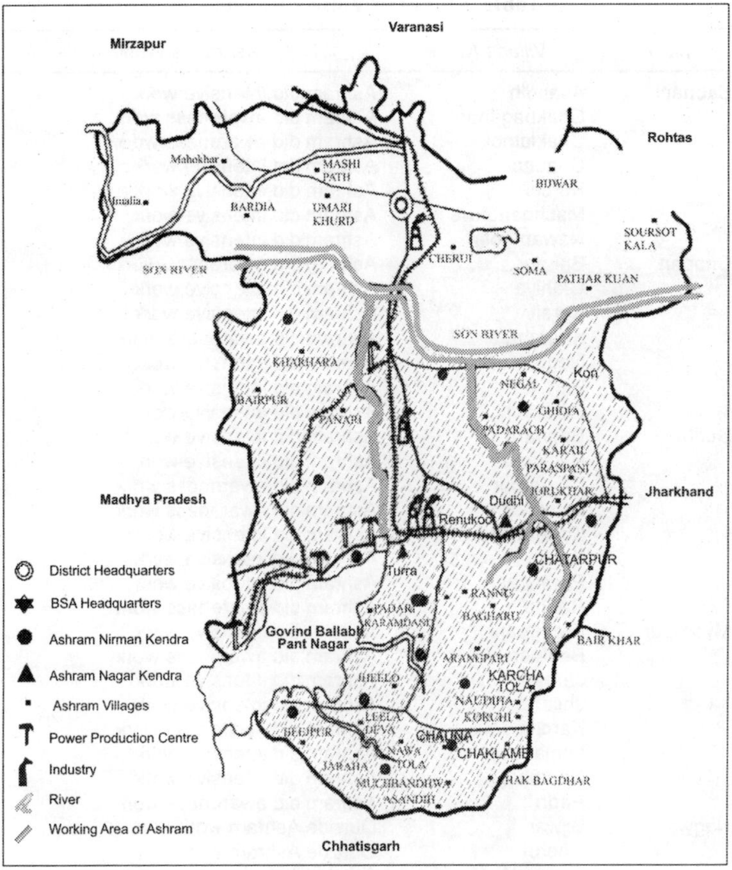

Map 2.1: Survey Villages

40 villages (Table 2.2). In the Ashram villages household listing covered one Gram Swaraj Sabha while in non-Ashram villages it covered the revenue village.

In the *third stage* 20 respondents were randomly selected for structured interviews. Half the respondents were males and half were females. Young people were also randomly selected from the household list and about 5 were interviewed from each village. Village Sarpanch was to be interviewed in each village. Table 2.3 shows the types of tools used for data collection and the sample size achieved.

Table 2.1: List of Villages Covered

Block	Village Name	Ashram's Work
Babhani	Asandih	Ashram did intensive work
	Chakbagdhari	Ashram did awareness work
	Chaklambi	Ashram did awareness work
	Chauna	Ashram did intensive work
	Korchi	Ashram did intensive work
	Machbandhwa	Ashram did intensive work
	Nawan Tola	Ashram did intensive work
Chopan	Bairpur	Ashram did awareness work
	Gidhiya	Ashram did intensive work
	Karail	Ashram did intensive work
	Kharahara	Ashram did awareness work
	Negai	Ashram did intensive work
	Panari	Ashram did intensive work
	Pararach	Ashram did intensive work
Dudhi	Bagharu	Ashram did intensive work
	Bairkhed	Ashram did intensive work
	Chatarpur	Ashram did awareness work
	Jorukhar	Ashram did awareness work
	Karamdand	Ashram did intensive work
	Karri	Ashram did intensive work
	Paraspani	Ashram did intensive work
	Rannu	Ashram did awareness work
Myorepur	Arangpani	Ashram did intensive work
	Beejpur	Ashram did awareness work
	Jarha	Ashram did intensive work
	Jhilo	Ashram did intensive work
	Karcha Tola	Ashram did awareness work
	Leeladewa	Ashram did intensive work
	Naudiha	Ashram did intensive work
	Padri	Ashram did awareness work
Nagwa	Bijwar	Outside Ashram work area
	Cherui	Outside Ashram work area
	Pathar Kuan	Outside Ashram work area
	Surarsot Kala	Outside Ashram work area
	Soma	Outside Ashram work area
Ghorawal	Bardiya	Outside Ashram work area
	Imiliya	Outside Ashram work area
	Mahokhar	Outside Ashram work area
	Masih Pathan	Outside Ashram work area
	Umari Khurd	Outside Ashram work area

Table 2.2: Details of Household Listing

Category	Ashram villages	Non-Ashram villages	Total
Blocks covered	4	2	6
Villages covered	30	10	40
Households listed	4509	1211	5720
Individuals covered	22167	6043	28210

Table 2.3: Sample Size Achieved

Data collection method	*Respondent Category*	*Sample Size*	
I. Structured Schedules	Adults		
	- Males	401	
	- Females	403	
	- Total		804
	Young People		
	- Males	100	
	- Females	101	
	- Total		201
	Sarpanch		40
	Health Worker		
	- ASHA	31	
	- Ashram Worker/Volunteer	8	
	- Jhola Chap Doctors	11	
	- ANM	1	
	- Dai	3	
	- Other	1	
	- Total		55
II. In-depth Interviews	Teachers		35
	Dai		5
	Faith Healer		5
	Ashram Workers		22
	Blacksmith		5
	Potter		2
	Barber		1
	Others		3
III. Focus Group Discussions	Adult (males)	33 nos	223
	Adult (females)	33 nos	220
	Adult (males)	6 nos	41
	Adult (females)	6 nos	44
	Ashram Workers	2 nos	24

In each of the survey village at least two FGDs were carried out. Interviews with Sarpanch, health workers and teachers were also carried out.

2.2 Characteristics of Respondents

Table 2.4 presents the characteristics of adult respondents and Table 2.5 presents the characteristics of young respondents. The data show that in the sample most adult respondents belong to Hindu religion, Scheduled Tribe (ST), agricultural workers as farmers or labour, earn between Rs. 2,000-5,000, and have very poor access to mass media — TV, radio or magazines. Almost all live in their own, *Kutcha* houses. The practice of open defecation is still present. Less than 10 per cent respondents have education level of High School and more. Young respondents are, however, drawn more from ST. About 80 per cent of them are literate and about 25 per cent are High School pass. All of them live in their own *Kutcha* houses. They too earn between Rs. 2,000-5,000 a month. They have a little better access to media. As compared to adults, the younger respondents also have better access to phones and mobiles. It may be noted that housewife's work is clubbed with no work. This is just to follow the tradition of surveys in India. This is also true that in the changing circumstances housewives too treat them as non-worker as they compare their condition of work with those actively working for money outside the family.

Table 2.4: Characteristics of Adult Respondents

Items	*Ashram Blocks*		*Non-Ashram blocks*		*Total*	
	No.	*%*	*No.*	*%*	*No.*	*%*
N	603		201		804	
Age (in complete years)						
Up to 19	0	0.00	1	0.50	1	0.12
20-24	1	0.17	0	0.00	1	0.12
25-29	82	13.60	35	17.41	117	14.55
30 or more	520	86.24	165	82.09	685	85.20
Average age	43.04 (13.20)		42.51 (13.78)		42.91 (13.41)	
Religion						
Hindu	588	97.51	194	96.52	782	97.26
Muslim	15	2.49	7	3.48	22	2.74
Others	0	0.00	0	0.00	0	0.00
Caste						
SC	84	13.93	38	18.91	122	15.17
ST*	355	58.87	79	39.30	434	53.98
OBC*	150	24.88	79	39.30	229	28.48
General	14	2.32	5	2.49	19	2.36
Family income (Rs per month)						
<1000	9	1.49	4	1.99	13	1.62
1,000 to 1,999	162	26.87	53	26.37	215	26.74
2,000 to 4,999	342	56.72	114	56.72	456	56.72
>5,000	88	14.59	28	13.93	116	14.43
Missing	2	0.33	2	1.00	4	0.50
BPL Status	269	44.61	85	42.29	354	44.03
Education						
Illiterate	358	59.37	124	61.69	482	59.95

Contd....

Table 2.4 *Contd.*

Items	*Ashram Blocks*		*Non-Ashram blocks*		*Total*	
	No.	*%*	*No.*	*%*	*No.*	*%*
Class 1 to 4	44	7.30	12	5.97	56	6.97
Class 5 to 7	63	10.45	29	14.43	92	11.44
Class 8 to 9	43	7.13	22	10.95	65	8.08
Class 10 & above	48	7.96	11	5.47	59	7.34
Informal education	47	7.79	3	1.49	50	6.22
Can read and write	217	35.99	70	34.83	287	35.70
Occupation						
Farmer	288	47.76	83	41.29	371	46.14
Agriculture labour	20	3.32	1	0.50	21	2.61
Other labour	100	16.58	48	23.88	148	18.41
Service	9	1.49	1	0.50	10	1.24
Artisan	7	1.16	1	0.50	8	1.00
Student	0	0.00	0	0.00	0	0.00
No work or housewife	158	26.20	54	26.87	212	26.37
Others	19	3.15	12	5.97	31	3.86
Missing	2	0.33	1	0.50	3	0.37
Marital status						
Unmarried	9	1.49	1	0.50	10	1.24
Married	563	93.37	188	93.53	751	93.41
Separated	2	0.33	0	0.00	2	0.25
Divorced	0	0.00	1	0.50	1	0.12
Widowed	26	4.31	11	5.47	37	4.60
Missing	3	0.50	0	0.00	3	0.37
House ownership						
Own house*	597	99.00	201	100.00	798	99.25
Type of house						
Kutcha	544	90.22	184	91.54	728	90.55
Pucca	28	4.64	8	3.98	36	4.48
Semi-pucca*	31	5.14	9	4.48	40	4.98
Satisfy with house*	327	54.23	76	37.81	403	50.12
Availability of clean water	332	55.06	116	57.71	448	55.72
Use of toilet						
Own toilet	16	2.65	1	0.50	17	2.11
Group toilet	1	0.17	0	0.00	1	0.12
Community toilet	3	0.50	0	0.00	3	0.37
Open defecation*	583	96.68	200	99.50	783	97.39
Have electricity	175	29.02	39	19.40	214	26.62
Ownership of gadgets						
T.V.	56	9.29	32	15.92	88	10.95
Phone/Mobile	323	53.57	118	58.71	441	54.85
Radio	122	20.23	29	14.43	151	18.78
Sewing Machine	31	5.14	9	4.48	40	4.98
LPG	12	1.99	4	1.99	16	1.99
Motorcycle	48	7.96	10	4.98	58	7.21

Contd....

Table 2.4 *Contd.*

Items	*Ashram Blocks*		*Non-Ashram blocks*		*Total*	
	No.	*%*	*No.*	*%*	*No.*	*%*
Car	2	0.33	3	1.49	5	0.62
Tractor	11	1.82	2	1.00	13	1.62
Thrasher	3	0.50	0	0.00	3	0.37
Tube-well	19	3.15	7	3.48	26	3.23
Read magazine						
Regularly	17	2.82	3	1.49	20	2.49
Sometimes	99	16.42	34	16.92	133	16.54
Never	487	80.76	164	81.59	651	80.97
Watch T.V.						
Regularly	17	2.82	9	4.48	26	3.23
Sometimes	92	15.26	23	11.44	115	14.30
Never	494	81.92	169	84.08	663	82.46
Listen to radio						
Regularly	64	10.61	10	4.98	74	9.20
Sometimes	155	25.70	48	23.88	203	25.25
Never	384	63.68	143	71.14	527	65.55

★ The difference between Ashram and Non-Ashram blocks is significant at 5 per cent level of significance.

Table 2.5: Characteristics of Young Respondents

Variable	*Ashram blocks*		*Non-Ashram blocks*		*Total*	
	No.	*%*	*No.*	*%*	*No.*	*%*
N	151		50		201	
Age (in complete year)						
15 to 17	26	17.22	9	18.00	35	17.41
18 to 20	35	23.18	17	34.00	52	25.87
21 to 23	57	37.75	15	30.00	72	35.82
23 & above	33	21.85	9	18.00	42	20.90
Average age	2.64 (1.00)		2.48 (0.99)		2.60 (1.00)	
Religion						
Hindu	149	98.68	49	98.00	198	98.51
Muslim	2	1.32	1	2.00	3	1.49
Others	0	0.00	0	0.00	0	0.00
Caste						
SC	18	11.92	7	14.00	25	12.44
ST	95	62.91	21	42.00	116	57.71
OBC*	33	21.85	17	34.00	50	24.88
General	5	3.31	5	10.0	10	4.98

Contd....

Table 2.5 *Contd.*

Variable	*Ashram blocks*		*Non-Ashram blocks*		*Total*	
	No.	*%*	*No.*	*%*	*No.*	*%*
Family income (Rs. per month)						
<1,000	0	0.00	0	0.00	0	0.00
1,000 to 1,999	35	23.18	9	18.00	44	21.89
2,000 to 4,999	97	64.24	29	58.00	126	62.69
>5000	19	12.58	10	20.00	29	14.43
Missing	0	0.00	1	2.00	1	0.50
BPL status	61	40.40	19	38.00	80	39.80
Education						
Illiterate	32	21.19	9	18.00	41	20.40
Class 1 to 4	8	5.30	2	4.00	10	4.98
Class 5 to 7	37	24.50	4	8.00	41	20.40
Class 8 to 9	38	25.17	15	30.00	53	26.37
Class 10 & above	29	19.21	20	40.00	49	24.38
Informal education	7	4.64	0	0.00	7	3.48
Can read and write	111	73.51	39	78.00	150	74.63
Occupation						
Farmer	35	23.18	6	12.00	41	20.40
Agriculture labour	28	18.54	1	2.00	29	14.43
Other labour	5	3.31	9	18.00	14	6.97
Service	6	3.97	3	6.00	9	4.48
Artisan	23	15.23	1	2.00	24	11.94
Student	47	31.13	14	28.00	61	30.35
No work or housewife	7	4.64	13	26.00	20	9.95
Other	0	0.00	3	6.00	3	1.49
Marital status						
Unmarried	46	30.46	18	36.00	64	31.84
Married	103	68.21	31	62.00	134	66.67
Divorced	0	0.00	0	0.00	0	0.00
Widowed	0	0.00	1	2.00	1	0.50
Separated	1	0.66	0	0.00	1	0.50
Missing	1	0.66	0	0.00	1	0.50
House ownership						
Own house	151	100.00	50	100.00	201	100.00
Type of house						
Kutcha	144	95.36	43	86.00	187	93.03
Pucca	3	1.99	2	4.00	5	2.49
Semi-pucca	4	2.65	5	10.00	9	4.48
Satisfied with their house	91	60.26	22	44.00	113	56.22
Clean water is available	97	64.24	31	62.00	128	63.68
Use of toilet						
Own toilet	2	1.32	0	0.00	2	1.00
Group toilet	1	0.66	0	0.00	1	0.50
Community toilet	0	0.00	0	0.00	0	0.00

Contd....

Table 2.5 *Cont.*

Variable	*Ashram blocks*		*Non-Ashram blocks*		*Total*	
	No.	*%*	*No.*	*%*	*No.*	*%*
Open defecation	148	98.01	50	100.00	198	98.51
Have electricity	45	29.80	17	34.00	62	30.85
Ownership of gadgets						
T.V.*	9	5.96	18	36.00	27	13.43
Phone/Mobile	101	66.89	38	76.00	139	69.15
Radio	39	25.83	18	36.00	57	28.36
Sewing Machine	17	11.26	3	6.00	20	9.95
LPG	3	1.99	4	8.00	7	3.48
Motorcycle	18	11.92	5	10.00	23	11.44
Car	3	1.99	1	2.00	4	1.99
Tractor	2	1.32	6	12.00	8	3.98
Thresher	1	0.66	2	4.00	3	1.49
Tube-well	5	3.31	6	12.00	11	5.47
Read magazines						
Regularly	12	7.95	10	20.00	22	10.95
Some times	47	31.13	17	34.00	64	31.84
Never	92	60.93	23	46.00	115	57.21
Watch T.V.						
Regularly	8	5.30	9	18.00	17	8.46
Some times	58	38.41	13	26.00	71	35.32
Never	85	56.29	28	56.00	113	56.22
Listen to radio						
Regularly	27	17.88	13	26.00	40.00	19.90
Some times	56	37.09	11	22.00	67.00	33.33
Never	68	45.03	26	52.00	94.00	46.77

* The difference between Ashram and Non-Ashram blocks is significant at 5 per cent level of significance.

2.3 Conclusion

This study enjoys a mix-method approach. The tools of the study include structured and unstructured interviews, FGDs and observations. In all, 6 blocks and 40 villages are covered in this study. 30 are from the area where Banwasi Seva Ashram is active and 10 are from the outside. A total of 5,720 households were listed and information was collected from 28,210 individuals. The characteristics of the respondents seem to be quite representative of the characteristics of the area. Thus in the sample most adult respondents belong to Hindu religion, Scheduled Tribe (ST), agricultural workers as farmers or labour, earn between Rs. 2,000-

5,000, and have very poor access to mass media—TV, radio or magazines. Almost all live in their own, *Kutcha* houses. The practice of open defecation is still present. Less than 10 per cent respondents have education level of High School and more. Within the limitations of the sampling design, the findings of the study seem to be generalizable to the entire area falling within the Ashram activities and outside.

CHAPTER 3

Community Organization

One of the major contributions of the Ashram has been to strengthen the institution of village panchayats. From the point of view of the Ashram, local organization of the village people, in the institutional framework of gram panchayats, was a key to the local governance. The aim was to promote Swaraj, meaning 'self-rule' and 'self-sufficiency' at the village level. Mr. Prem Bhai and other leaders of the Ashram thought that Gram Swaraj was an essential step towards empowerment of people. They thought that to launch struggles of the oppressed, especially the tribal who were ignorant, fatalist and vulnerable due to isolation and exploitation by outsiders, it is essential that they are involved in planning for themselves. The tribals were backward from the outsiders' perspective. However, they had a well developed society; their own quite evolved differentiation and integration. The founders of the Ashram recognized that for a long time streams of warriors came to take shelter in the forests, when attacked by foreign invaders, and living together they had developed a well integrated model of village society. Different tribes and groups specialized in different arts, crafts and productive activities and for many a purpose they took collective decisions. The idea was that it is only when villagers develop a sense of community, they would be able to resist exploitation in the hands of moneylenders, power brokers, and the state, and instead they will be able to plan for their village, consensually and collectively. The leaders were inspired by Mahatma Gandhi and Vinoba Bhave. Vinoba Bhave had said:

> Let us move from village to village and ask the people to think of the good of the village. They should sing the glory of their village. Glory to every village will mean glory to the country. When every organ of the body functions well, the body as a whole functions well....... All the departments that we have at the national level should be there in every village. Every village should look after industries, agriculture, health, education, justice etc. and should, therefore, have arrangement for the same.

In this model of local self-governance, which was proposed much before the Panchayati Raj Act came into existence, a three tier structure was developed in the Ashram villages:

- Gramswarajya Sabha (GSS) is the 1st tier which has all families as members. The general body elects its Secretary and President.
- Kshetriya Gramswarajya Sabha is the 2nd tier which has representation of each GSS. The presidents and secretaries of GSSs are its members and it is served by a Village Development Centre. Typically 5 to 6 villages come under a Village Development Centre and it acted as an information centre collecting and disseminating information to villagers.
- Kendriya Gramswarajya Sabha is the 3rd tier and has representation of Kshetriya Gramswarajya Sabhas and the Ashram's own development departments.

It may be noted here that this three-tier system came into existence out of necessity because of the local people's constraints in mobility and free time. The services had to be brought closer to them. Eventually, this system, built out of necessity, proved to be a solid and trustworthy institutional set up, consistent with the Gandhian philosophy of independent village republics.

3.1 Institutional Development

The first GSS came into existence in 1958. At present 445 GSSs are functional in 230 revenue villages. The Ashram developed Vikas

Manch which is a forum of 4 to 6 neighbouring villages. There are 80 Vikas Manchs and 13 Gram Nirman Kendras. At the Vikas Manch level the Ashram placed a Swaraj Sathi who helps in organising people in each GSS and create awareness amongst the villagers. There are 66 Swaraj Sathis who form an important link between the Ashram and villagers. At the Vikas Manch level there are Swastha Mitras, Pashupalaks (livestock experts) and a Gram Sakhi. At present there are 160 Swastha Mitras, 10 Pashu doctors and 181 Gram Sakhis. The Gram Sakhis work with local women and take up issues pertaining to women including women empowerment, health and nutrition.

Photo 3.1: A scene of the annual Gram Swaraj Sammelan held at Govindpur, 2011

The GSSs take up the planning activities at the village level with active participation of people. These plans are presented to the panchayats. In the words of Shubhaji "this is a forum for development of people where politics and religion (i.e. factional and sectarian considerations) have no place. This is what people want." GSSs hold regular monthly meetings and discuss issues pertaining to their own village. Villagers support GSS because this is the only trusting forum where they can set their own agenda.

3.2 Dispute Settlement

The Gram Swarajya system has brought in peace and harmony in villages. Now in most cases people would not run to law courts but resolve their differences at the village itself. According to the Annual Report of Banwasi Seva Ashram, during the year 2010-11 a total of 87 dispute cases were handled and 52 cases were settled by GSSs. Earlier, during 2009-10 about 187 cases were presented to GSSs, out of which 154 were settled. This reflects people's trust in the GSS representatives and faith in the panchayat system. Most of these cases pertain to land and water drainage disputes (with neighbours), problems caused by stray grazing of animals, family feuds, and husband-wife conflicts The disputes are settled through mediation by members of GSSs and the elected representatives, who are deemed to be fair-minded and unbiased. As opposed to this, in the non-Ashram villages there is no such mechanism available for people and hence they rush to the courts for settling all kinds of cases.

In the words of Dr. Ragini Prem, "The disputes get settled at the village level itself easily as the two parties sit together and talk to each other. These decisions are, therefore, more acceptable to people. We are in the neighbourhood of Naxal affected area. For years Naxals made attempts to make in-roads into our villages also, but they did not succeed. The reason is that there are hardly any grudges people have with each other that relate to land settlement."

3.3 Representation of Women

The meeting of GSSs are well attended by men as well as women. There is also a good representation of women in the programmes that are conducted by GSSs. A large proportion of women attend the annual meetings of Vikas Manch, which is held at the Ashram. Between October 2009 and September 2010 there were 187 meetings for dispute settlement at GSS level in which 894 women and 1,544 men participated.

It is notable that in 10 GSSs, the Swaraj Sathi is a woman. In fact a large number of secretaries and presidents of GSSs are women. Table 3.1 shows the percentage of GPs with women Sarpanch at the time of the survey. In blocks like Babhni the representation of women is particularly high. At 48.39 per cent it is much higher than the 33 per cent reservation made for women. However, in the two blocks, outside the Ashram activities, Ghorawal and Nagwa also the women are well represented among the village Sarpanchs. Yet, fieldwork shows that women Sarpanchs of the Ashram area are more aware and active as compared to women Sarpanchs outside who are guided by their husbands for most decisions.

Table 3.1: Women Representation in GPs

Blocks	*Number of Gram Panchayats*		
	With women Sarpanch	*Total Gram Panchayats*	*%GP with women Sarpanch*
Babhni	15	31	48.39
Chatra	19	48	39.58
Chopan	22	51	43.14
Dudhi	17	45	37.78
Ghorawal	44	112	39.29
Myorepur	27	65	41.54
Nagwa	18	45	40.00
Robertsganj	38	104	36.54
Total	**200**	**501**	**39.92**

Source: District Panchayati Raj Office, District Sonbhadra, 2011.

3.4 Representation of SC/ST

It was a horrendous task to bring the downtrodden into the mainstream of the village life. Efforts were made to raise the participation of lower castes and tribal groups in the organization of panchayats. Thus today people of all castes and communities are well represented in the village institutions promoted by the Ashram. Data show that out of 66 Swaraj Sathis 10 are from SCs, 36 are from STs, 12 are from OBCs and only 8 are from the Other Castes. Overall there is a high representation of SCs and STs in the institutions of Ashram.

3.5 Participatory Planning and Programme Monitoring

The foundation laid by the Ashram promoted village level participatory planning and cooperation. The GSSs are prepared to develop the capacity to make plans for the village. The study shows that many of the GSSs made plans and pursued them with the Gram Panchayats. During the year 2008-09 eight GSSs were successful in getting their plans included into the government run planning processes initiated under MNREGA.

It is sad to observe that over the years some of these participatory traditions have weakened. More than a quarter of GSSs are not as active any more as they were. The result is that villagers are not keen to attend Gram Sabha meetings and perform community works. Some of the concepts as of labour bank have discontinued as people rush to seek work under MNREGA or out-migrate. As compared to the formal panchayat system the Ashram has no resources to distribute among people. Still walking through the villages under the Ashram activities one finds glimpses of the rich tradition of cooperation:

1. GSS acts as a pressure group wherever a mishandling of projects is reported. Swaraj Sathis get involved in works such as getting job cards and ration cards made for the local people. In Kachnerwa panchayat (block Chopan), Awadhesh Prasad is a Swaraj Sathi. He received complaints from people that a contractor has been engaged in the village to construct road and he (the contractor) is not using boulders. Rather he is mixing soil and sand. Awadhesh Prasad immediately collected evidence with the help of villagers and reported the matter to the SDM. Consequently, the things were corrected. Voices like that of Awadhesh Prasad are being raised from all over the places.
2. In Murta village (Dudhi block) there were around 25 labourers who were not given the wages earned under MNREGA for more than one year. The issue was raised at the GSS meeting. Immediately, Jagat who is a Swaraj Sathi, called at the Help Line of MNREGA. When the district administration did not respond for two weeks, he filed a

complaint on the Tehsil Diwas. In another fortnight the payments were made. The villagers have begun to understand their rights and how they can go about handling a situation when there is injustice and corruption.

3. In Panari village (Chopan block) the panchayats started making a dam to hold rainwater. The work was left incomplete as the funds dried up. 300 men and women of the village got together and decided to complete the work. They worked collectively and completed the work. Today more than 20 acre land got irrigated with this dam.
4. For researchers who have worked on rural development in different parts of the country, this comes as a surprise that in the Ashram area villagers get their community hand pumps fixed themselves. They do not wait for PHED engineer or their Sarpanch to do this work. The tradition of collecting funds and celebrating festivals is still alive. These are small steps that reflect the cooperative thinking of the people.

3.6 Forest Rights

For a long time the Ashram had been launching a scheme called Rural Entitlements and Legal Support Services (REALS) which was drawn up with the active cooperation of Justice P.N. Bhagwati and Dr. Rajeev Dhavan. According to Hoddy, "Prem Bhai's main concern was to nip conflicts in the bud before they took a violent turn." The Ashram helped in setting up REALS in the States of Bihar, Madhya Pradesh, Orissa, and other areas of Uttar Pradesh, outside Mirzapur district (Hoddy, 1999). In 1986, the Ashram started meeting people at the village level and formed the Bhoomi Haqdari Morcha (BHM). Under BHM the Ashram mobilized people to conduct *dharnas* (sit-ins), and put up road blocks at a number of crucial junctions. The tribals squatted on the road and halted traffic on a total of 93 km of roads. The Government used force and removed the tribals from roads and started terrorising them. However, this helped in two ways: the movement drew attention of journalists, lawyers, civil rights activists and others who came to Sonbhadra, saw the justness of the claims of people and wrote that the State Government was flouting the Supreme Court directives on the laws of the land. This also made the tribal people realize that if they are united they were very powerful. Their fear of police and administrators vanished. They rejected the age old superstition that going to prison is tantamount to losing caste.

The passage of "The Scheduled Tribes and Other Traditional Forest Dwellers (Recognition of Forest Rights) Act, 2006" has been a landmark decision that gave legal rights over landholding to those settled in forests before December 2005. The process to be adopted for judging the claim involved setting up a Forest Rights Committee in each village. The villagers were to elect 10-15 committee members from the local residents. The committee was to initiate the process of verification of rights and place its recommendations before Sub-Divisional Level Committee and to be finally approved by a District Level Committee. It was in June 2008 that the district administration of Sonbhadra hurriedly, and in a clandestine manner, formed these committees overnight. This would have worked against the interests of the intended beneficiaries of the Act, the tribal and forest dwelling communities. The Ashram opposed the formation of such pseudo-committees immediately by organizing a movement to oppose the process of committee formation. The movement initiated by the Ashram continued unabated for several years. Finally, in October 2008 the District Magistrate of Sonbhadra took the decision to dissolve the existent Forest Rights Committees and form fresh committees. Thereafter the Ashram took an intensive programme to make people aware about the processes to be adopted for verification of land records.

The data collected through the adult schedule show that in the villages and blocks where the Ashram was active, the level of awareness about the Forest Right Committees has been higher. Nearly 57 per cent of the adults in the Ashram blocks knew about the presence of this Samiti as compared to only 26 per cent in the non-Ashram blocks. The highest awareness was found to be in the Myorepur block, in which the Ashram is located.

However, from the point of view of the Ashram functionaries the battle is far from being over. Several cases are yet to be settled. The Act recognises up to four acres of land, yet the majority of tribal people have not received that much land. The issue is on anvil.

Table 3.2: Awareness of Respondents about Formation of Forest Right Committee

Block	*Yes**		*No*		*Don't Know*		*Total*	
	nos.	*%*	*nos.*	*%*	*nos.*	*%*	*nos.*	*%*
Ashram blocks	346	57.48	52	8.64	204	33.89	602	100.00
Babhni	71	50.71	24	17.14	45	32.14	140	100.00
Chopan	79	56.43	9	·6.43	52	37.14	140	100.00
Dudhi	92	57.14	12	7.45	57	35.4	161	100.00
Myorepur	104	64.60	7	4.35	50	31.06	161	100.00
Non-Ashram blocks	54	26.87	75	37.31	72	35.82	201	100.00
Ghorwal	25	24.75	40	39.60	36	35.64	101	100.00
Nagwa	29	29.00	35	35.00	36	36.00	100	100.00

* The difference between Ashram and Non-Ashram blocks is significant at 5 per cent level of significance.

3.7 Conclusion

The study reveals that Ashram paved the way for the development in the region which was unreachable for in the past. It developed a three-tier, decentralized system of rural governance much ahead of state. Through this decentralized system the Ashram was able to implement its people-centric interventions for integrated development of the region. Funds and programmes were channelized through Ashram and people designed their own village development plans. The Ashram brought people together, empowered the vulnerable sections of society, and created a cultural context in which all castes and tribes, rich and poor, and males and females could work together. The people of this backward region, who were cut-off from the mainstream development, understood their rights and cooperatively fought for it. This has been a major contribution of Ashram.

Five decades later, the Ashram villages appear to have been affected by changes in the outside world. The institutions formed by the Ashram only stand as a parallel structure to the PRI system. Much more funds are moving into the area, and they are channelized through PRI system. The role of GSS is reduced to that of a pressure group. In the last 7 to 8 years the region also suffered a series of droughts, which led to a spurt in out-migration. While some went away in search of livelihood, others chose to work for MNREGA.

This has left little space and recognition for village planning and collective action. The institutions built by the Ashram have weakened in some places and their volunteers have experienced sagging morale. However, in spite of what the situation is right now, one thing is clear that due to efforts of the Ashram the local people have developed capabilities that are not easy to find. They can still sit and put their heads together to decide what they want in their village, make a development plan, and choose a course of action for the future. Their institution can usher the road to decentralised village level planning as was envisaged in the Panchayati Raj system. Under the leadership of the Ashram people still come together and ask for their rights.

CHAPTER 4

Education

Banwasi Seva Ashram has been working for over 50 years in the four blocks of Sonbhadra and made several interventions in education. For the Ashram education was a vehicle of development, social integration and self-reliance. With this idea, the Ashram established hundreds of pre-schools, primary schools, junior high schools and high schools. In addition, there were night schools for working children, informal schools for adults and *balwadis* for children aged 1 to 3 years. Most of these schools have been closed down now except one High School which is located in the Ashram premises and five Junior High Schools. There is also a vocational training centre within the Ashram premises which offers short term courses on rural technologies that are popular in the region. This chapter presents the findings of the study on educational interventions of the Ashram, and the story of their successes and failures. At the end it also touches upon the other activities launched by the Ashram towards information and communication.

4.1 Need to Set up Schools

In early sixties, the time when the Ashram started its activities in the region, illiteracy was widespread. Due to ignorance tribals were robbed of the state benefits they were entitled to and were exploited by moneylenders. It was clear that literacy of people has to be one of the most important agenda of development programme, empowerment and mobilization. Therefore, Prem Bhai conducted a detailed survey of all primary schools. Ram Awatar, an old associate

Photo 4.1: A village school

of the Ashram, recalls how people used to go on foot from village to village for data collection. Some villages were so remote that it took three to four days to reach there. The data were manually compiled. The results were shocking and the status of education was found to be dismal. These results were shared with state government so that the attention of the government could be drawn towards the need for providing education in the area.

There were two types of schools in the region. Some schools were run by the erstwhile princely state, while a number of schools were run by government, known as Parishadiya Vidyalaya. It was found that most of the government schools existing in the area were closed or defunct. Immediately a strategy was chalked out to create pressure on the government to make the existing schools functional and effective. However, the Ashram realized that this alone would not be enough. Therefore, the Ashram took up the task of setting up new schools with a whole new approach to learning and education to meet the needs of the people.

The Ashram first started its education programme with adult literacy and mobile literary programmes. Because there were no schools, and people could not afford expenditure on education, the Ashram opened schools with the support of child sponsorship projects—some in Govindpur under direct managment and some in remote areas.

The Ashram schools were to serve as a model for government schools. Ram Awatar adds, "Looking at the Ashram schools functioning, government teachers felt ashamed and came under pressure to be present in school to teach. In this area, the Ashram presented a functioning model of education to government and earned trust of the local people." The intervention worked.

4.2 Approach

The educational programme was designed on Gandhian principles. Dr. Ragini Prem states:

> A good educational programme shall combine acquisition of knowledge with craft-work because true education of the intellect can only come through a proper exercise and training of the bodily organs. Unless the development of

Photo 4.2: Girls in an Ashram School

> the mind and body goes hand in hand with a corresponding awakening of the soul, as stressed by Gandhiji, the former alone would prove to be a lopsided affair. By education, he [Gandhi] meant an all-round drawing out of the best in child and man's body, mind and spirit. From the beginning the Ashram believed in this strongly.

The Ashram spearheaded a movement in this region with a clear philosophy. In the words of Dr. Ragini Prem, "With education a person should better understand himself or herself, understand his or her society and people, and understand to live with nature." The Ashram used this gospel to design its educational programmes. Practical training was rendered to help people become economically self-sufficient. The techniques of teaching were inspired by Nai Taleem promoted by Gandhiji, according to which the students come to schools not only for education but in schools they also learn a skill and work to make them self-sufficient.

Thus in the Ashram schools timetables were chalked out so that children sought classroom lessons, and also carried out productive work. Farming, weaving, tailoring, carpentry, pottery and other crafts were integral part of the school curriculum. Children were taught lessons through gainful work that they could easily relate to. Initiating educational programme in drought stricken area where people were struggling for survival was a challenge for the Ashram workers. In a discussion Ram Sajeevanji, who was associated with schools said to the interviewers: "We told villagers that they must learn to make signature so that no one can exploit them. They must learn to write their name and family members' names." The teachers were planned to be appointed from the village people. In most villages it was difficult to find even a single educated person. Therefore, some teachers were sent from Govindpur. And thus the process started.

In Navatola village of Babhni block, villagers recounted their experiences when the Ashram started its first school. The teachers were so dedicated that they sat under a tree and started teaching. Villagers too helped out and soon a school building was constructed. There was a liquor distiller close to the school, which was closed down due to pressure from villagers. *The school united the whole village.*

4.3 Growth

Many new ideas were tried out to spread literacy. Educational programmes started with functional literacy in 1967-68, and continued at a substantial scale for years. Next intervention was setting up of Night Schools for working children. This was a condensed course for classes upto 5th standard. Next new programme was Morning School, for children of 3-6 years age group. In the later years special efforts were made for increasing female literacy. While the Ashram conducted several drives and ran programmes, it never planned regular schools on a large scale.

The schools were set up based on the demand of the villagers. Villagers donated land and helped in construction of buildings. The involvement of parents in setting up and running of schools was matchless. Vimalji, an old functionary of the Ashram, recalls how in 1978 the Ashram had started a night school and a Gram Shala. This all started with conducting a survey of the parents to gauge their interest in education. The idea was that nothing should be imposed from outside, not even education. Moticharan of Joru Khera (Dudhi) told that as a child he worked in the daytime, and took animals for grazing in the evening and in the night he would attend the school. He was too excited to go to the Ashram school. There were problems and resistance. Some people spread the rumour that the Ashram is planning to conduct family planning programme and will forcibly sterilize the males. The school attendance declined immediately. Actually, two years before, during the Emergency period people were coerced to get sterilized and the issue was so sensitive that the next parliamentary elections were held mainly on the issue of compulsory sterilization. It took a lot of time to convince them that the Ashram is not associated with family planning programme. Once that happened, the children returned to the Ashram schools. Teachers were supposed to meet parents every week and keep updated about children's progress at home. Teachers had a very high morale, a very high commitment. Vimalji says he remembered names of all 200 students in his school. So was the case with the other teachers of the Ashram.

During the period 1990-96 Total Literacy Campaign (TLC) was launched with support from UNICEF. Three years later, Children

Science Congress and Life Education Programme were added. When the Ashram workers noticed that several children join their parents in these classes, separate classes were started for them. Bal Mandirs or day schools for children up to the age 6 and Gramin Shalas or night schools for the working children were opened to meet the needs of different sections of society. The Gramin Shalas offered a condensed programme of three years during which pupils were brought to Class V level. Later on, a High School was started in Govindnagar itself which offered hostel facilities to students. At some of the Village Development Centres Primary and Junior High Schools were started. All these schools were opened with support of villagers who were involved in setting up and running of schools. The Ashram was declared District Resource Centre for the Total Literacy Campaign.

In the words of one of the retired teachers of the Ashram, "villagers quickly saw the benefit of education given by the Ashram teachers. Villagers from all over the region started calling the Ashram to set up a school in their village."

Today all these programmes have been discontinued except one High School and five Junior High Schools. Continuation was not possible for want of finances and because there was an expansion of government programmes for primary education. Now Ashram holds camps for young boys and girls. They are called life orientation camps. The Ashram also conducts vocational courses for electricians, mechanics and several other categories of workers.

4.4 Impact of Educational Programmes

Ashram ushered a new era in Sonbhadra by making education accessible and attractive to each and every household. The assessment of the impact of such a programme is a difficult task as the programmes are now shrunk to a few camps and schools. The following discussion attempts to capture the data and stories people narrated to the researchers that provide us with their perspective of impact.

4.4.1 Literacy Rate

Table 4.1 shows the trend in literacy rate in Sonbhadra district. The data are taken from Census of India, 2011 and pertain to age group 7+.

Table 4.1: Literacy Rate by Sex, 1991-2011

Sex	*1991*	*2001*	*2011*
Male	37.79	63.06	77.19
Female	14.36	33.80	54.11
All	26.94	49.32	66.18

The above table shows that the literacy rate in Sonbhadra district has made a significant jump in the last two decades. The overall literacy rate which was 26.94 per cent in 1991 rose to 49.32 per cent in 2001 and 66.18 in 2011. The increase in female literacy has been even more impressive. In two decades Sonbhadra has come a long way. When villagers were asked why they want education, they said in chorus: "without education we will be backward. We want good education for our children." In forty years of the Ashram interventions the situation has changed.

Teachers of the Ashram School as well as the ordinary villagers narrate with pride the success stories of students. After seeking education in the Ashram schools some became school teachers, BDC and Shiksha Mitra, and many have set up their own business. A school principal said: "There is no dearth of our alumni who are doing social work. Many of them are elected members of Panchayati Raj now as Panch or Pradhans."

Shri Ram is Sarpanch of Jarha village (Myorepur). He fondly remembers walking to the Ashram school at Govindpur with his fellow village children. "Whatever I am today, I can largely attribute to the teachings of the Ashram."

4.4.2 The Alumni Entrepreneur

Zia-ur-Rahman, 34 year old tailor, got his education at the Ashram School at Manbasa (Dudhi block). He enjoyed tailoring classes in the school. The home science teacher gave the first lesson of stitching in Class VI, followed by cutting and sewing. After completing his High School education, Manoj (or Zia-ur-Rahman) moved to Robertsganj to work. Soon he returned back to his village to set up his own tailoring shop. Tailoring was also his paternal occupation. Today he is quite happy and his shop on the roadside offers enough work to him and his three assistant tailors. In the last Gram Panchayat elections, he was elected as a member of Gram Panchayat.

4.4.3 Untouchability

As said above, for the Ashram education was also a means of social integration. Using education as a vehicle of transformation, the Ashram was able to address the problems of social evils like untouchability. The Ashram had a strict policy of non-discrimination based on caste, class or gender. In Jugail village when the school started, people of higher caste opposed sitting of their children on the same mat with children belonging to Harijans (Scheduled Castes). The Ashram schools gave them no choice and promoted mixing of all castes and communities both inside and outside the school. According to Shubhaji, "The situation was quite bad. The Harijan could not pass by the homes of upper caste people with an umbrella on their head. This was the situation till the year 2002, but it is not to be found anywhere now." Today when WIZMIN team arrived in the village, there were people of all castes, both males and females, who intermingled with each other with ease.

4.4.4 Career in Education

Shiv Mangli is a Shiksha Mitra at Government Primary School, Manbasa (Myorepur block). She studied at Ashram School in Manbasa, and later lived in hostel at Govindpur to complete her High School education from the Ashram School. Her parents got her married soon after that. When she was looking for work, the Mission School quickly made her an offer. Shiv Mangli had worked as Supervisor in the Adult Literacy Programme of the Ashram for a few years. With three small children, she completed her intermediate education and joined a degree college for graduation in arts subjects. Subsequently she got appointed as a Shiksha Mitra (under government education programme).

4.4.5 Girls Education

Padri is a progressive village today but four decades back here the literacy was very low. Jamuna Prasad Yadav, Sachiv of Van Sanrakshak Samiti, says: "Hamare gaon mein shiksha ka deepak Ashram ne jalaya" (in our village the lamp of education was lit by the Ashram.). The Ashram distributed books and set up mobile library. The household survey of the village shows that out of 122 girls, only 17 have not been enrolled. Rest of them attend school. Today 10 to 20 girls come out to live in Govindpur Ashram and carry out further studies.

The Ashram paid special attention to education of girls. When the Ashram started its activities no girl went to school. Today more than half of the class in a typical school comprises of girls. One old man recalls that earlier girls were not allowed to go out of village, even for studies. Now hoards of girls can be seen in places like Dudhi where they live in rented rooms or hostels to study. Although this change cannot all be attributed to the Ashram activities alone—the other forces of change are also responsible—but in the initial days the Ashram played a vital role in promoting girls education and fighting against the gender discrimination.

4.4.6 Education and Culture

One of the major strengths of the educational model of the Ashram was that it instilled self-confidence amongst people who joined formal or informal education activities of the Ashram. Instead of promoting the formal education, it looked for indigenous practices and traditions, and carefully weaved them with the classroom lessons. The students who came out of these schools were supposed to be much more aware about their traditions and much more in harmony with surroundings. This response can be heard from numerous villages of southern Sonbhadra: "The children who went to Ashram schools are cultured. They respect their teachers and elders. They have appreciation for traditional dance and songs. They are quick to volunteer their time and effort for any village work. This is what makes them different." In a society where government education has been so well ingrained, the educational initiatives of the Ashram were innovative and praiseworthy.

4.4.7 The Current Scenario

The current situation is very different. Government has created a vast network of schools. These schools also provide mid-day meals, stationary, dress and scholarships. In order to reap these benefits parents are tempted to enrol their children in government school though they are not happy with the quality of teaching there (as they were with Ashram schools earlier). To quote Kusum Devi, Sarpanch of Karamdand (Dudhi block), "The Ashram schools were good. In government schools the standard of education has fallen down. The Ashram schools focused on teaching and learning, the government schools are focused on mid-day meals and meetings alone."

Vishwa Mitra Kushwaha, Shiksha Mitra of Jorukhad (Dudhi block) says: "Now the children are not getting training to do traditional work like weaving. The type of education they get makes them unfit to work in the village. When they do not get work locally they run away to Surat and Mumbai to work as labour. When Ashram school was here, children learned more useful things in short time." Clearly, they feel need for providing that type of education which is related to the context and which promotes traditional arts and craft.

The comments of villagers comparing schools of Ashram with that of Government schools reflect on the achievements of Ashram.

Ashram run schools	*Government run schools*
The Ashram taught useful things like better agriculture techniques, composting, etc.	Government school teachers are doing business with students (i.e., collecting money for private coaching, passing them in exams etc.
There was good discipline.	Young people are loosing sense of respect for elders.
The Ashram connected to our roots and customs.	Now it is all English culture (*Angrezi*).
Teachers taught us in the night, using lantern.	Teachers are passing time in school. They are not interested in teaching.
More things were taught in the Ashram schools, and fees was less.	Fee is less and so is the educational content.
Teachers used creative ideas to teach. They were some of the things we cannot forget.	The new education is mostly bookish.
Teachers knew us and our families personally; they knew our problems and often helped us also.	Teachers are transferred every now and then.
The Ashram taught everyone how to sign; it was due to their efforts that in a short period most people could read.	The quality is so low that even a Vth pass child is unable to read.

The educational infrastructure has expanded but the schooling system is in disarray. There is a shortage of teachers. The teachers do not come to school regularly. Quality of education is poor and students go missing. When a team of researchers visited the GPS, Jharokhur, they found that out of 173 children only 68 were present. When Narendra Prasad, a Shiksha Mitra was asked he said: "Parents are not taking interest in education. They load girls with household work and many boys work at brick kiln. Some children fill as proxy as several of them go for MNREGA work. They miss out at school. Once they lag behind, their performance goes down and eventually they drop out. In this village everyone in ten children is a drop out and/or out of school." The education that is rendered today is bookish and students do not learn how to do things with their own hands. The paternal occupations are fast disappearing. Prem Prakash, a cobbler by profession, states: "Boys of our caste have of course started going to school now. But after that they are shifting away from our traditional work of leather craft. 15 boys of our family recently left for Chennai to work as fitter and do the shuttering work."

4.5 Information and Communication Activities

The survey shows that although in the initial days the Ashram provided substantial material support to the villagers, including food, work and agricultural inputs, the major contribution of the Ashram lies in raising awareness, mobilising people and connecting them to experts/labs and new knowledge. Yet, the situation is fast changing. The connection between farmers and people is no more so intense. Table 4.2 shows that as of today villagers seek information about agriculture from various sources. Among them family appears to be the biggest source of information. It is surprising that very few respondents now seek information from the Ashram, though in the Ashram area, they admit, that once it was a major source of information and inspiration. The younger generation of people shows a reduced enthusiasm for the Ashram activities. Obviously the Ashram cannot compete in the field of rural and tribal development with the government's policies and programmes which has enormous resources and support for its programmes at all levels.

Table 4.2: Source of Information

Source of information	Ashram Villages		Non-Ashram villages		Total	
	nos.	%	nos.	%	nos.	%
Learnt from family members	487	47.33	156	42.86	643	46.16
Friend, neighbour or relative	310	30.13	136	37.36	446	32.02
Officials of KVK, agriculture department	48	4.66	19	5.22	67	4.81
Ashram workers	89	8.65	0	0.00	89	6.39
TV, radio, newspaper, magazine	63	6.12	29	7.97	92	6.60
SHG or CBO	1	0.10	0	0.00	1	0.07
Other	31	3.01	24	6.59	55	3.95
Total responses	1029	100.00	364	100.00	1393	100.00

4.6 Sustainability of Efforts

Withdrawal of funding by outside, particularly from Christian Children's Fund and Aid as well as fall in local support, led to serious problem. The Ashram made special efforts to guarantee schools' survival by creating reserve fund and involving the people. When the Balwadi project got closed, some villagers started coming forward to run the Balwadis. Ganesh Prasad at Babhni Kendra took the initiative of running the Balwadi himself. However, with a few exceptions there is a lack of initiative and it is becoming difficult to sustain the education initiatives of the Ashram.

The household listing data show that the Ashram villages do not carry the legacy anymore (Table 4.1). It is disheartening to note that in terms of school enrolment the villages where the Ashram carried out intensive work, have faired worse than the non-Ashram villages. More than one-quarter of the people below age 18 years have either dropped out or never enrolled. The situation of girls is even worse. For example, in Bairpur village (Chopan block) the Ashram carried out several programmes including education. At present 77.2 per cent women of this village reported that they never went to school. Around 40 per cent men also never studied in any school. A similar situation was seen at the Ashram villages in Manbachwa, Chauna, Karamdand, Rannu and Bagharu where 18 to 20 per cent girls are out of school. Here the Ashram once had its own school, Night School and Total Literacy Campaign (TLC). The programmes, after Ashram left, could not sustain for long.

Table 4.3: Status of Education by Gender and Work of Ashram

(Per cent of respondents below age 18 years)

Status of education	*Villages where Ashram did Intensive work*		*Villages where Ashram only did Awareness work*		*Villages where Ashram did not work*	
	Male	*Female*	*Male*	*Female*	*Male*	*Female*
N	3764	3295	1764	1543	1469	1318
Enrolled	50.5	46.3	51.8	48.7	53.6	52.8
Dropped out	7.9	6.1	8.6	6.4	5.7	2.6
Never enrolled	14.4	21.8	15.4	17.7	14.0	15.0
Too young	27.3	25.8	24.1	27.2	26.7	29.4

There is tremendous frustration among the teachers who once taught in the Ashram schools. They, of course, worked voluntarily and drew only a small honorarium. But they treated this honorarium as their salary and thought that their work will continue forever or as long as they want. Closure of the Ashram schools has come as a great shock to some of them. This shows the limits of voluntarism if the voluntary institutions depend on outside funds. The funds can be withdrawn or diverted any time to other activities and the project stops.

4.7 Conclusion

It is a complex issue to explore what is the Ashram's contribution towards spreading education. In the early days the Ashram spread awareness about the importance of education in the isolated, tribal parts of the district. The Ashram also created a vast network of schools which imparted good quality education with involvement of local people and volunteers. This produced good results. However, as time passed, when state government started creating a number of primary and secondary schools, the Ashram schools started becoming dysfunctional and getting closed down. Yet, people still remember the contribution made by the Ashram schools and how at one time they provided a model of well functioning school, putting moral pressure on government teachers also to perform.

The efforts made in the field of education were not sustainable. While the programmes ran for two to three decades, and people received good, value based education and availed its benefit, they did not come forward to run the Ashram schools on their own. For some the efforts could have been more sustainable if the Ashram handed over responsibilities to government at the right moment and in a right manner. But the two efforts, the Ashram efforts and the government efforts, were made in independent manner with disregard for synergy. The Ashram used the participatory approach to education; the government used the delivery approach without special concern for quality or integrated development of the area as the aim. In this process the Ashram model of education could not be sustained. Experience shows that in poverty stricken areas there is a limit to evolve non-governmental, self-supporting model of education itself which could compete with or guide the government action. However, one cannot blame the Ashram. In the process Ashram has created a huge set of resources—trained teachers, teaching tools and an understanding of local culture. At present the Ashram stands as a beacon in Sonbhadra that everyone looks up to. In a way it is better positioned to be a Learning Resource Centre that can train teachers of government schools, roll out innovative teaching tools and develop relevant curriculum. In the future organizations like the Ashram are more suited to develop Learning Resource Centres than formal schools. It is for the government to take the advantage of the Ashram.

CHAPTER 5

Agriculture

At the time the Ashram started working in Sonbhadra area of the then Mirzapur district, the area lacked in irrigation facilities and agriculture was largely dependent on monsoon. A large number of jungle streams and rivers (Rihand, Kanhar, Bijul and Pandu rivers) cut through the land. Land around these streams and rivers is undulated, rock-filled and eroded. The soil is coarse, filled with

Photo 5.1: Ravinous land near Kanhar river in Dudhi Block

gravel and has poor water retention. In this part of the state monsoon has always been erratic and it posed a great difficulty before the farmers. Majority of people here survived on subsistence agriculture and several of them were completely or partially dependent on forest produce. Looking at the frequent onslaught of drought and acute shortage of grains in the region, the Ashram took up 'food for work' and intensive agriculture work on a priority basis. An integrated watershed development work appeared to be important to the Ashram so that the rainwater could be harvested in reservoirs, to be made in every village. In this context, watershed, land development and improvement in agriculture practices formed the core of the Agrindus project.

5.1 Major Agricultural Activities Promoted by Banwasi Seva Ashram

As mentioned above, the first set of work was to carry out watershed and land development activities. For improvement in agriculture, a demonstration farm was developed and efforts were made to make farmers aware about improved agricultural practices. In addition, livestock development, afforestation and horticulture were also promoted. Farmers were given the confidence to experiment with new methods and at the same time keep faith in the time tested traditional wisdom they possessed. Some of the major activities taken up by the Ashram are discussed below.

5.2 Watershed and Land Development

In the sixties the land development work was the mainstay of the agricultural interventions. Under the 'Food for Work' programme, land levelling and bunding works were taken up first. This was done at a large scale during 1967 to 1975. Land was terraced, levelled and bunding was done to hold water in the fields. Approximately 1,200 acre land was taken up during this period for land improvement, benefiting more than 800 farmers.

During 1966-67, the Ashram dug up nearly 200 wells and this number increased to 1,800 by 1991. Due to lack of electricity and capital *Rahats* (animal driven water wheels), *Bandhis* and hand held tube wells were promoted. While *Rahats* were not reported to be so successful, each *bandhi* could irrigate approximately four acre land and benefit three farmers. Bunds were made on individual and community land, benefiting thousands of farmers. The Ashram workers showed people how to level the land, and how to prepare fields for efficient production of wheat, paddy and vegetables.

Photo 5.2: Irrigation tower at the demonstration farm of Banwasi Seva Ashram, Govindpur

Looking at the results, gradually all 400 project villages followed the suit. Farmers were given diesel pumps and were encouraged to take up intensive farming. ***Lift irrigation tower was a special innovation of the Ashram.*** Such towers were constructed in several villages. Under this system, water was first lifted up using a pump and then with the help of laid down pipes it was taken to high land. The efforts of the Ashram produced good results. Today this area has thousands of earthen dams, hundreds of irrigation towers and irrigation wells.

While in the initial phase the entire cost of such projects was borne by the Ashram, the assets were maintained through ensuring farmers' active participation. The concept of Labour Bank was introduced in several villages, and is still prevalent at some places.

5.3 Demonstration Farm

The Ashram was given 250 acre land by UP Government. At the time of the grant this land was undulated and infertile. The Ashram selected 160 acre of this land and developed it as a demonstration-cum-production farm. This land was levelled, *Bandhis* were built and water was harvested, irrigation channels were constructed, and new crops were tried out leading to diversified agriculture. People from the Ashram and nearby villages toiled under the leadership of Prem Bhai and developed it as a green oasis. Villagers were surprised to see that fruits and vegetables could be produced on the fallow land. So far they had thought that if at all anything could be produced on this land the land was suitable for cultivation of coarse grain only. Later organic farming also was demonstrated to people. *Bandhis* and irrigation towers were first experimented here before they were propagated in the wider project area. This experiment served as a successful model for villagers who could see and get inspired to develop their own land. This not only instilled a confidence amongst villagers, this also provided an experimental and learning ground for agriculture extension workers who came here from other district of the state and other states to see new innovations in agriculture.

5.4 Livestock Development

Tribal people depend on forests and animals. They keep plenty of animals and use them for farming and cow dung. Traditionally there was no awareness of vaccination and their cows did not have good yield of milk. They did not store fodder for animals and left them free for open grazing in forests and fields (*era pratha*). The Ashram realised that this system destroys a good part of their crop. Moreover, summer time animal mortality was quite high because of shortage of food, fodder and water. Animals also suffered from various diseases during the rainy season. Mortality of animals was reported to be very high but the government provisions of veterinary services hardly existed in the area.

The Ashram took up several initiatives for the livestock development. The goal of the Ashram was to increase milk production, introduce better quality animals with higher disease resistance, and improve the general health of the livestock. In 1970 the Ashram started procuring good quality cows from outside — Ganga Tree breed from Allahabad, and cross bred cows from Indore and Panipat. Under Agrindus project the Ashram started a dairy farm and procured different breeds of animals. It then promoted crossbreeding and encouraged people to have dairies, which later became a supplementary source of their income.

In the next phase stress was placed on increasing availability of fodder for animals. Villagers were told to save stalks of maize and other crops for fodder, and were encouraged to grow green fodder for animals. Fodder seed was distributed to farmers free of cost. Some villagers were encouraged to open a fodder depot that made fodder available during the lean season.

Photo 5.3: Desi breeds of animals in Karri village of Dudhi Block

As mentioned above, there was a big lacuna in veterinary service. The Ashram decided to work in close cooperation with the government and started training local people in animal breed, health and illness, and feed. Soon there was a set of people ready to look after the health of animals, give them vaccination and assist in artificial insemination.

In addition to the above, following programmes were also taken up:

- Since 1976 exposure visits were organised for veterinary services to the National Dairy Research Institutes (NDRI), Karnal (Haryana), Bareilly (UP), Anand (Gujarat) and Chandrapur (Maharashtra). This continued till 1990 and many people got training to provide veterinary services locally.
- During the period 1980-90 Kamdhenu Yojana was taken up in which good quality cows were distributed to farmers. Around 200 farmers in four blocks got benefited.
- Artificial insemination was started in 1980. However, it did not meet much success.
- Cattle fair was started since 1982 to promote availability of good quality animals. This fair is still held annually at the Ashram *Mode* (turn). Over the years enough private participation has come in its organization.
- In 1995 the Ashram started castration of animals using scientific method. The traditional practices prevalent at that time were painful and cruel to animals.
- Dairy extension programme during 2003-2010 was taken up to promote animal fodder, fodder storage and distribution of fodder seeds; insemination centres, vaccination centres and milk collection centres were started to promote marketing.
- Since 2003 a team of more than 40 voluntary service providers and veterinary *Vaids* (traditional practitioners) are ready in villages for veterinary services. They provide free service to the villagers and charge only for the medicines. In addition, they also hold regular meetings with farmers and create awareness amongst villagers on the following points—(1) contagious diseases and vaccination, (2) protection from cold, (3) care of infants, (4) scientific

method of sterilisation, (5) colostrums, (6) protection from insects, ticks and pests, and (7) fodder cultivation and management.

- Training of veterinary *Vaids* was held in 2009 at the Ashram on disease prevention and control.

5.5 Farm Practices

Traditionally, in the tribal belt people were used to growing millets and coarse grains only. Lack of efficient practices and lack of irrigation facilities were the problems. With the efforts of the Ashram, land was levelled and more irrigation water was made available. Now the farmers learned to grow paddy and wheat. Vegetable growing and kitchen gardening were also initiated by the Ashram. Today tomatoes, cauliflower, beans, and brinjals are widely cultivated. In each house one can see a small orchard. Cultivation of bamboo, jackfruit, mango, lemon and *aonla* trees is commonly seen in the area. The Ashram also promoted cultivation of medicinal plants like turmeric, *neem* and *tulsi*. People were encouraged to develop *badi* (vegetable garden) at their homes and increase consumption of fruits and vegetables.

Photo 5.4: A kitchen garden in Satbahani village (Block Babhni)

Bhola, a 70 years old farmer of village Faripan remembers that earlier people only used broadcast method of sowing. The Ashram taught them sowing in a row that led to much better productivity. Several such initiatives were taken up by the Ashram.

Table 5.1 shows that in the Ashram villages significantly lesser land (68.33%) is irrigated as compared to the non-Ashram villages (79.10%). This is because of lack of irrigation facilities, poverty, poor quality of land, and a relative neglect of the area. Yet, in spite of that orchards and vegetable gardens have been more popular amongst households living in the Ashram villages. Outside the house having a few fruit plants, bamboo and bean creeper is a common site in these villages.

Table 5.1: Popularity of Orchards and Vegetable Gardens

Item	*Ashram villages*		*Non-Ashram villages*		*Total*	
	No.	*%*	*No.*	*%*	*No.*	*%*
N	603		201		804	
Farmers with irrigated land*	412	68.33	159	79.10	571	71.02
Farmers who have an orchard	127	21.06	23	11.44	150	18.66
Farmers who have vegetable garden	151	25.04	37	18.41	188	23.38

* The difference between Ashram and Non-ashram blocks is significant at 5 per cent level of significance.

5.6 Gram Vikas Kosh

Poverty stricken and tribal dominated villages of the Ashram lacked in credit. The only source of the credit outside family and relatives was loan from moneylenders who would charge exorbitant interest on the loan and also use loan for various other forms of dominance, exploitation and oppression. There were no banks, no roads, and no government. In this context, the Ashram established Gram Kosh fund at the time Agrindus project was started. The concept was to develop fund at the village level with small contributions made by the local people. Some of the infrastructure maintenance activities and small loans to villagers were funded through this Kosh (fund). Thus each GSS had its Gram Vikas Kosh which gave loans on the norms similar to those of other financing institutions permitting a

10-year term for irrigation and land development programme, three years for purchase of bullocks and one year for assistance by way of seed and fertilisers. This generated lot of village participation and vibrancy in different development programmes. A study showed that hundreds of families were benefited with this Kosh. For the year ending June 1979, farmers had repaid 64 per cent of the amount due on irrigation, 72 per cent of the amount due on purchase of bullocks and 82 per cent of the amount taken for seeds and fertilisers. Although all the sample households had taken loan from Gram Kosh, the loan was used mostly for productive purposes; the number of people taking consumption loan and loans for social obligations significantly reduced. According to another study by Agriculture Finance Corporation assistance through Gram Kosh was extended to 100 villages in the area.

As it happened to education programme of the Ashram, at present the concept of Gram Vikas Kosh has become dormant. At some point of time the voluntaristic spirit was lost. Those who took loan, did not repay. The intensity of development work also reduced, and so were the contributions to the Kosh. The great setback to Gram Vikas Kosh was the fight for land right which involved expenditure on settlement of individual cases, application proofs, appearance in courts, and the expenditure on travel.

5.7 Land Improvement

The major impact of the Ashram has been in changing the face of the area. As some old people recall, the land levelling was done at a very large scale. Ravines were reclaimed and land was terraced and levelled. During an FGD in Padrach village (Chopan block) Ramasre recalls, "this green field and *bandha* that you are seeing now was jungle before 1970. There was a *nala* flowing through and land was all uneven. Now you can see that land is beautifully levelled. Rainwater is still there in the *Bandhi* in the month of May, and farmers around here use it to irrigate their fields. The Ashram people themselves got involved and made water channels. Slowly everyone around here copied it. Now this farm gives us enough rice for the whole year. Earlier we had to buy for at least 6 to 7 months."

Photo 5.5: Lata, a manual water lifting device from well using a wooden lever is quite popular in villages of Sonbhadra

Table 5.2 shows that compared to those outside the Ashram a larger proportion of respondents in the Ashram villages said that land development work had been taken up in their fields. When they were asked who did the work, in the Ashram villages one quarter of the respondents stated that it was done by the Ashram.

It is interesting to note that in the Ashram villages 42.29 per cent respondents reported that the land development on their farms was ever done while outside the Ashram only 26.37 per cent respondents reported the same. In a quarter of cases in the Ashram villages this work was done by the Ashram.

Table 5.2: Land Development Work

Land development work	*Ashram villages*		*Non-Ashram villages*		*Total*	
	No.	*%*	*No.*	*%*	*No.*	*%*
N	603		201		804	
Per cent respondents on whose fields land development work was done*	255	42.29	53	26.37	308	38.31
Agencies who did land development work						
– Self*	124	40.00	39	65.00	163	44.05
– Government project	108	34.84	21	35.00	129	34.86
– Ashram	76	24.52	0	0.00	76	20.54
– Others	2	0.65	0	0.00	2	0.54
Total responses	310	100.00	60	100.00	370	100.00

* The difference between Ashram and Non-ashram blocks is significant at 5 per cent level of significance.

Note: On the villages where the Ashram did Intensive work, 46.9 per cent of the respondents said that land development work was done in their fields as compared to 33.0 per cent in Awareness villages and 26.4 per cent in non-Ashram villages.

5.8 Improvement in Irrigation

With the efforts of the Ashram the land got consolidated, levelled and area under irrigation jumped up significantly. There are several success stories of land bunding and water harvesting, and people taking ownership of the work. The table below shows clearly that in the Ashram villages a larger area has been irrigated by *bawalies*, ponds and check dams constructed by villagers themselves to harvest rainwater. On the other hand the non-Ashram villages have a higher dependence on canal and tube wells (Table 5.3).

The two year old bund of Panari village (Chopan block) was destroyed under the force of water. The Sarpanch refused to get it repaired. Balendraji tells, "Sarpanch said that there are no funds at this point of time". The villagers got together and decided to repair it themselves. About 300 villagers including more than 100 women came forward. Women lifted the soil while men did the digging work. For one week they all worked together. This bund is now

Table 5.3: Method of Irrigation

Item	*Ashram villages*		*Non Ashram villages*		*Total*	
	No.	*%*	*No.*	*%*	*No.*	*%*
Method of irrigation						
Canal*	6	2.08	39	34.5	45	11.19
Bawali/Pond/Check Dam*	125	43.25	20	17.7	145	36.07
Well/Tubewell	95	32.87	47	41.6	142	35.32
Others	63	21.80	7	6.2	70	17.41
Total	**289**	**100.00**	**113**	**100.0**	**402**	**100.00**

*The difference between Ashram and Non-ashram blocks is significant at 5 per cent level of significance.

Photo 5.6: Water harvesting structure at Panari village made by the community

irrigating close to 25-30 acre land, and animals come here to take bath.

5.9 Use of Bullocks for Ploughing

The Ashram had promoted country plough as a better method of tilling than tractor. The survey shows that there is a significantly higher ownership of bullocks and wooden *hals* (ploughs) in the Ashram villages than outside. However, there is no significant difference in the ownership of tractors and threshers between the Ashram and Non-Ashram villages (Table 5.4).

Photo 5.7: Bullock ploughing

Table 5.4: Comparison of Ploughing Methods in Ashram and Non-Ashram Villages

Ownership	*Ashram villages*		*Non-Ashram villages*		*Total*	
	No.	*%*	*No.*	*%*	*No.*	*%*
Farmers who have a bullock* (*Source*: Adult schedule)	443	73.47	117	58.21	560	69.65
Ownership of *hals* per household (*Source*: Sarpanch schedule)	0.88		0.72		0.86	
Ownership of tractors (*Source*: Adult schedule)	11	1.82	2	1.00	13	1.62
Ownership of thresher (*Source*: Adult schedule)	3	0.50	0	0.00	3	0.37

* The difference between Ashram and Non-ashram blocks is significant at 5 per cent level of significance.

5.10 Promotion of Orchards and Vegetable Gardens

Old people stand witness to the improvement in agriculture and jump in farm output. Villagers learnt to grow vegetables and develop orchards at home. Improved agricultural practices such as row sowing were introduced. People started growing herbs such as turmeric for home remedies. Several farmers adopted irrigation towers.

Photo 5.8: Row sowing being done by women in Arangpani village (Block Myorepur)

Photo 5.9: Cultivation of turmeric in Rannu village (Block Dudhi)

5.11 Increased use of *Desi* Seeds and Organic Farming

The indigenous or *desi* seeds appear to be loosing battle against hybrid seeds except in some pockets like that of Sonbhadra where farmers have realised the virtues of *desi* seeds. The Ashram has taken special interest in motivating farmers to continue to use and improve upon *desi* (local) seeds. *Desi* varieties of crops are more appropriate in the natural surroundings of the area, especially in the dry land, and for the season these seeds are not to be purchased from outside. Ashram's extension work has kept in halt movement towards hybrid seeds and chemical pesticides, herbicides and fertilizer. The survey shows that 74.46 per cent of the respondents in the Ashram villages prefer to use *desi* seeds as compared to 35.82 per cent in the non-Ashram villages. Common farmers do realise the ill effects of hybrid seeds. As Dhanman in Auradandi village puts it, "Hybrid seeds are going to make our bodies sick. It makes our soil sick also". Responses of several other farmers, in the box below, show why they prefer to use *desi* seeds.

BOX 5.1: WHY USE THE "*DESI* SEEDS"

1. Crop using *desi* seeds gives better taste.
2. Grains using *desi* seeds are better for digestion and nutrition.
3. *Desi* seeds can be preserved for the next year while hybrid cannot be preserved.
4. Hybrid seeds are more expensive.
5. Hybrid seeds need more fertilisers and water.
6. Crop matures faster if *desi* seeds are used.
7. Hybrid seeds need to be bought every year.
8. Crops with *desi* seeds have more hay, which is useful for animals.
9. Crops with *desi* seeds are more pest resistant.
10. For this soil (low water retention), *desi* seeds are more suitable
11. *Desi* seeds can be borrowed from and shared with others in the village.
12. Hybrid seeds are not good for soil because they harm growth of friendly earthworms.
13. There are many varieties of local seeds (*desi* seeds) and this promotes diversity.

Munni Devi is an active and aware woman aged 35 years. She and her husband have been associated with the Ashram for quite some time. She regularly attends the village level meeting held by the Ashram. She has only 2 bighas of land which is irrigated through Lata. In her village Rannu (Dudhi block) there are many other farmers who have switched to hybrid seeds and chemical fertilisers. However, Munni Devi and her family have resisted this force of change. She says: "hybrid seeds eventually come out to be more expensive because we need to buy them every year. Hybrid seeds also demand more urea which is not a good thing to use. Urea reduces the strength of our soil". She prepares a desi concoction using bahaya leaves, urine of cow, gur and uses it as pesticide. She knows how to preserve desi seeds in earthen pots for use in following year. She says she learnt these methods from the Ashram workers only.

Nevertheless, common people are getting tempted to use hybrid seeds due to their promised attractive yield. As Buddhan Bhai puts it, "earlier the *desi* varieties were there with a lot of hay. The hay of *Kodo* was a pleasure for animals. Now, it is not to be sown. Hybrids are dwarf in nature and give very little straw. Animals do not relish the taste of its fodder."

5.12 Use of Green Manure

A walk through the Ashram villages shows a larger sensitivity of the natives for nature and green practices. Meetings and conferences held at the Ashram and extension work done by the volunteers have definitely produced results. People realise the value of organic farming, and there are several villages where by and large people have shunned use of chemical fertilisers and pesticides. According to the *District Statistical Bulletin* (2009) the usage of chemical fertilisers in the Ashram blocks is 64.6 kg per hectare as compared to 176.6 kg per hectare in the two non-Ashram survey blocks.

> Ram Lochan is a young farmer of Faripan (Myorepur block) who is a strong advocate of organic farming. He has been greatly influenced by the teachings he got from the Ashram. He tells that till four years back he was himself using chemical fertilisers. In the beginning the yield increased. But soon the soil started turning hard, and the yield started

> declining. He frequently visited the Ashram farms and observed the agricultural practices used there and learned the benefits of organic farming. He set up composting unit, as taught by the Ashram. Now he stopped using chemical fertilisers all together and grows organic vegetables. The cauliflowers, brinjals and tomatoes grown by him with green manure fetch good price in the market.

The table given below shows that percentage of respondents in the Ashram villages who prefer to use organic manure and organic pesticides is higher than the same outside the Ashram. Although the percentage of farmers who go for crop rotation is higher in the non-Ashram villages than in the Ashram villages but the difference is not statistically significant. This shows that with the indigenous varieties of farm inputs too the Ashram village farmers are able to do as well as the farmers outside.

Table 5.5: Sustainable Agricultural Practices

Item	*Ashram Villages*		*Non-Ashram Villages*		*Total*	
	No.	*%*	*No.*	*%*	*No.*	*%*
N	603		201		804	
Farmers who prefer organic manure*	331	54.89	23	11.44	354	44.03
Farmers who prefer organic pesticides*	158	26.20	10	4.98	168	20.90
Farmers who do crop rotation	209	34.66	72	35.82	281	34.95

* The difference between Ashram and Non-ashram blocks is significant at 5 per cent level of significance.

Several testimonials and stories are there reflecting the understanding of people.

> Faripan is a progressive village of Myorepur block where the Ashram has a Nirman Kendra. Ram Lochan Gaur is 30 years old and has 4 acre land. Around 1994 he started using urea in his fields. He enjoyed the increase in yield of wheat and potato for good three years. But soon he started observing the ill effects of chemical fertiliser—the soil seemed to have become harder making ploughing tougher.

> Gradually the yield started reducing, and the year rainfall reduced, he suffered a big loss and could not recoup the investments he had made.

Around the same time he was told by the Ashram how to prepare compost on farm and was given a chance to travel to Maharashtra in early 2009. He saw farmers doing organic farming with which he was highly impressed. The same year he allotted 10 Biswa land for organic farming. Now he reduced urea in paddy, and his vegetables farming is 100 per cent organic. He saw that when he used organic manure, the crop was not affected by pests and vegetables were tastier. To prepare organic manure he had dug up trenches in which he collects cow dung, soil and hay, and covers them with leaves. Then they are covered with mud and allowed to rot for a three to four months.

Slowly the effect is rubbing on others in the village. This year 15 more farmers tried growing organic vegetables.

BOX 5.2: WHY USE ORGANIC MANURE?

1. Cow dung is available at home.
2. Need for chemical fertilizer keeps on going up every year.
3. Cow dung is good when there is a shortage of water. Chemical fertilisers require lots more water.
4. Urea reduces soil strength and crop yield declines after a few years.
5. Chemical fertilisers are expensive.
6. The good effect of cow dung manure remains in soil for several years (about ten years).
7. Chemical fertilizers are very potent and kill the taste of food.
8. Use of cow dung manure makes crop more pest resistant.
9. No upfront cost is required for home made cow dung manure.

5.13 Increased Use of Organic Pesticides

The Ashram gave demonstration on making organic pesticide which could be used as an alternative to chemical pesticides. "Use of *Angrezi dawa* in agriculture *makes the people unhealthy, the soil also looses its health,*" says Ram Prasad. He makes organic pesticide using Bahaya leaves, gur, urine of cow and cow dung.

This mixture is left for chemical processing for a few months till it is ready for spraying on paddy leaves. It is claimed to be very effective for paddy and wheat. Many farmers have taken inspiration from the Ashram and experimented with this on their farms.

5.14 Afforestation and Improvement in Biomass

Efforts of a long period of afforestation are beginning to produce results. In the dry land also the survey team witnessed a large expansion of greenery. The case of Jarha village (block Myorepur) may be pointed out here. The residents of this village were once displaced from Singrauli. When Singrauli dam came up in sixties, hundreds of families were given land here. This village was situated in the middle of a forest. Slowly people cut down trees and started cultivation. Rajkumar lives in the village and remembers that by 1970 three quarter trees of the forest were felled. The pollution created by National Thermal Power Corporation (NTPC), Beejpur plant adversely affected the natural habitat. By the end of eighties there was hardly any forest left.

Photo 5.10: The green hills of Padrach village is a result of efforts made by villagers and specially women

This is when the Ashram started its afforestation activities here. The Ashram went for awareness drives and distributed saplings of eucalyptus, bamboo, *aonla*, mango, guava and *neem*. The Ashram did plantation in the individual farms of 16 farmers, and some on community land. Rajkumar tells that he got so much interested in plantation that he started buying saplings from the nearby nursery. Looking at the greenery on his fields, others in the village also started afforestation.

Padrach village (Chopan) is on Kaimur hill range surrounded by rivers Kanhar and Son. People of older generation recall when they were growing up how thick greenery once existed there. Continuous felling of trees, with the connivance of forest officials, eroded the hills completely.

With the awareness drives of the Ashram, there has been a change in the collective consciousness of people regarding their environment. During one FGD Bandhu Prasad said, "*hame apna jal, jangal aur janwar bachana hai* (we have to protect our water sources, forests and animal)". In a similar vein, Rameshwar Prasad says: "No outsider will come and help us if we do not help ourselves". The spirit caught on and villagers formed a *sangathan* (association). Women came forward in large numbers. They opposed cutting of trees on their hills. Their actions did not fetch them fame as in case of Chipco or Appico women but their struggle and their determination were not less than those of women known for participation in ecological movements outside. And in many respects they are successful too. With pride, Ram Vilas shows how green and picturesque now their hills are as compared to the hills of other villages.

5.15 Improved Livestock

Traditionally, livestock has been as important to village economy as agriculture. Yet, due to poverty, lack of resources, lack of knowledge and lack of modern veterinary health facilities, the life and quality of their livestock was rather poor. As mentioned earlier, due to the efforts of the Ashram, livestock vaccination was well accepted. The survey shows that 65.3 per cent of the respondents in the Ashram villages got their animals vaccinated as compared to 54.7 per cent in the non-Ashram villages. This is a significant achievement that should reduce the morbidity and mortality in the livestock population.

Table 5.6 shows that while the concentration of bullocks and goats is higher in the Ashram villages, milch animals are somewhat more in the non-Ashram villages. Bullocks are used for ploughing and goats for milk and flesh. In rural economy of UP goats are poormen's substitutes of cows/buffaloes.

Table 5.6: Differences in the Concentration of Livestock in Ashram and Non-Ashram Villages

Animals	*Ashram villages*		*Non-Ashram villages*		*Total*	
	No.	*Animals per family*	*No.*	*Animals per family*	*No.*	*Animals per family*
N	603		201		804	
Cows	602	1.00	278	1.38	880	1.09
Bullocks	975	1.62	238	1.18	1213	1.51
Buffaloes	66	0.11	95	0.47	161	0.20
Goats	1235	2.05	128	0.64	1363	1.70
Other animals	371	0.62	78	0.39	449	0.56

Two years back the Ashram organised a meeting of *Vaids* (traditional health practitioners) who are interested in treating animals using herbs. This was a useful get together in which people shared information with each other. Shobhan Ram Yadav is a livestock *Vaid*. He says: "The Ashram promoted the practice of not leaving animals stray for grazing and taught people to save their hay for animal fodder. Today the milk production has increased significantly though the number of animals per family has reduced. Surely the quality of livestock and their health has improved."

Shyam Bihari is a beneficiary of the livestock programme of the Ashram. He says, "Earlier none of us got our animals vaccinated. On the behest of the Ashram, *Vaids* got trained and they started visiting villages. Now everyone accepts vaccination. The Ashram workers also promoted production of *Berseem* (green fodder)."

5.16 Sustainable Development

In practical terms sustainable development requires that the villages become self-reliant for most of their needs. This was the dream of Gandhiji that for both agricultural and non-agricultural needs (like textile) the villagers are self-reliant and independent. With various initiatives taken by the Ashram, in general, farmers learnt to reduce their dependence on outside sources. The faith in traditional practices of using indigenous seeds got accepted and home made organic manure became popular. This resulted in reduced cash need for farmers. The responses of Sarpanchs on how dependent their farmers are on outside sources for their seed and fertilizer requirements are quite encouraging. More people in the Ashram villages understood that by using *desi* seeds and organic manure, they will be less dependent on outside resources.

Table 5.7: Dependence of Village on Outside Sources for its Seeds and Fertilizers Need

	Ashram villages		*Non-Ashram villages*		*Total*	
	No.	*%*	*No.*	*%*	*No.*	*%*
Village is independent	11	36.7	0	0	11	27.5
Village is dependent*	19	63.3	10	100	29	72.5

* The difference between Ashram and Non-ashram blocks is significant at 5 per cent level of significance.

Note: In case of Saghan villages 40 per cent are independent, in awareness villages it is 30 per cent.

Source: Sarpanch Schedule.

The Ashram changed agricultural practices in the project areas. It provided people with information that helped them understand benefits of traditional practices, and at the same time learn new techniques. There is a big history of experimenting, learning and revising in the work done by the Ashram. However, the modern development is posing a big challenge to the tasks taken up by the Ashram. Hybrid seeds and chemical fertilizers are making in-roads quite rapidly. Changing lifestyle and out-migration of young people has caused reduction in animal stock. The large varieties of coarse grains and millets have nearly disappeared. Forests are

BOX 5.3: VIRITUES OF DESI SEEDS

Nigai (Block Chopan) is a tribal village inhabited mainly by the people of Kharwar community. This small village of 70 families is tucked behind a hill, 10 km away from the main road. Though disconnected from main stream development, people are smart enough to reject chemicals fully in their village. The Ashram workers have been quite active in this village. People understand that *desi* seeds are more suitable for them. When four years back a company made promotional offer of hybrid seeds to farmers, seeds of maize and paddy was given to farmers free of cost. The company also held promotional camp and explained to farmers how to cultivate using hybrid seeds.

Soon the villagers realized that hybrid seeds required much more inputs—more urea and more water. They had observed how in the water deficient season some crops simply dried up. Farmers understood the benefits of *desi* seeds and organic farming. Mr Jagdish Kharwar reports: "The hybrid rice was tasteless. Who wants it?" Farmers switched back to *desi* method. They realised that use of hybrid seeds requires more expensive inputs. Today barring one or two farmers, everyone in this village makes cow dung manure and uses *desi* seeds. Harishanker, the Ashram worker says: "People here are close to nature. They know the virtue of keeping bullocks".

Photo 5.11: Green pastures of Nigai village that largely practices organic farming

not protected by law and the result is that dry fruits like *chironjee*, which were at one time staple diet of the tribal people here, have just disappeared.

Modernity promotes speed and farmers of Sonbhadra are also looking for quick results. Akhilesh Chandra Dewedi, Teacher, Government Middle School, Medhnikhad laments: "Now *Kodo*, *Sawan*, *Medu* and *Bajra* had disappeared from our plates. Even production of *Urad*, *Moong* and *Til* (Sesame) is fast reducing because they do not grow on urea. They require organic manure. Bullocks are getting replaced by tractors. *Chironjee*, *Chakwar* and *Mahua* was part of our regular diet. Trees are there but they refuse to produce them. The whole environment is disturbed. Mother nature is angry with us." Today the Ashram is finding it difficult to counter the force of modernity. More and more villages are under its trap. People want quick results. They are less concerned about the community interests or the future. For example, the Ashram worked hard in Padri (a village of Myorepur block) to make people aware about virtues of traditional methods of farming and using *desi* seeds. Dineshji was a school teacher in an Ashram school and was an active member of the Ashram. He is a Swaraj Sathi. Contrary to survey team's expectations, his son, Jag Jeevan who was given hybrid seeds to sell by some external seed company and who runs a shop, tried to experiment with the hybrid seed of paddy and bought urea for his three acre land. He was happy with the results and promoted it amongst other farmers. His farm was used by a seed company to demonstrate their seeds. Now 35 farmers are using the same hybrid seeds. Today Jag Jeevan advertises for this company and he gets a commission from them.

A significant change that took place in the last few decades is a steady decline in the production of millets. *Kodo* millet (*Paspalum scrobiculatum*), *Sawan* millet (*Echinochloa frumentacea*) and *Bajra* or Pearl millet (*Pennisetum glaucum*) formed staple diet of people. This also had very high shelf life. Millets are suitable to the soil and climatic conditions of Sonbhadra as they adapt to poor, droughty, and infertile soils. With the introduction of wheat and paddy, the millet production went down.

5.17 Conclusion

In sum, the Ashram has played a key role in agricultural development in the project area. Initially, the Ashram took up land development and watershed programmes. New techniques of wasteland agriculture were developed raising yield and land under agriculture. The Ashram then initiated livestock development programme and showed how the two programmes have a synergistic relationship. In the later years Ashram promoted the time tested local traditional practices, organic farming and use of *desi* seeds, manure and pesticides. Seeing Ashram in the lead, people could understand the virtue of organic farming.

However, in the changing circumstances, the Ashram faces daunting challenges ahead. Under the effect of modernization and government schemes the farmers are shifting to new practices. Although they realize that from the sustainable development point of view the traditional fertilizers, seeds and pesticides were better but for quick gains they have started using chemical fertilizers, high yield variety seeds and chemical pesticides. The concept of Gram Kosh discontinued. The Ashram cannot stop the influence of change. Sustainable agricultural practices need an ideological substratum. Westernization (change of values), individualization and need for money are posing serious threat to the Ashram activities. More and more people are confused. After tasting some development on various fronts they are unwilling to go back. And yet, they also see the big risks ahead. They seem to be in need of sustainable, self-reliant, community based model of organic farming but modernization, materialism and possibility of migration prevents them from thinking collectively and sustainably.

CHAPTER 6

Crafts and Village Industries

Gandhiji believed in the revivification of India's villages through the development of village industries. Founders of the Banwasi Seva Ashram also realised that while farm income will remain the primary source of income for village people, village industry and crafts need to be promoted to provide additional support, and also help in preserving the cultural diversity of people. Tribals were already skilled at producing handicrafts which served their functional and aesthetic needs. Bamboo work, woodwork, metalwork and herb processing were part of their life. The crafts and arts were interwoven with the culture and religion of the people. For example, the Panikas of the village weaved saris specially designed for the bride. Similarly, the pots made by village potters formed part of auspicious items required in marriage ceremony.

Village economy in this area was well integrated: the tribal villages had the tradition wherein villagers paid a portion of their agricultural produce as revenue while its craftsmen received a stipend out of the crops at the harvest time for their services. In this interdependent economy, villages were economic units and were mostly self-sufficient. People also helped each other in other activities such as house construction and house modification. Dr. Ragini Prem, commenting on the lifestyle of the tribal family in Sonbhadra, said: "Houses in our villages are *kutcha*. Tiles (*khaprail*) making and woodwork is done artistically, and almost all the households know how to do it. When it is time for someone to repair roof (*chappar chavani*) people of the entire village would get together and help out. No mason and carpenter is hired from outside. The lifestyle and tradition have been built around mutual cooperation." In this backdrop, development of village and khadi industry was a logical course that the Ashram followed. The approach was that handicraft and village industries will help build village economy, make it independent, and develop villages into self-sustaining units.

6.1 Analysis of the Decay of Traditional Industry

Working in the Gandhian framework, the Ashram observed that modernization and industrialization are posing the major threats to traditional crafts and village industries. There are several reasons: some related to demand side and some to supply side. On the demand side, villagers are now exposed to factory made goods, and slowly demand of home spun cloth and hand made pots is reduced. On the supply side, the Ashram felt that in modern India the traditional crafts have received a raw deal due to which they are unable to maintain their production levels. The state policies have been such that the sources of raw material became inaccessible to artisans. Tribals lost access to forest produce like bamboo, wood, grass and other minor forest produce. They suffered the loss of resources as they were highly dependent on forests for raw materials, medicines, food and fodder. Some herbs and plants started disappearing due to over exploitation of land and ill effects of modern industry.

Atarilal, a bamboo worker of Khairahi village (Myorepur block), complained: "We were stopped on roads by the forest officials who accused us of committing theft. We were often caught by the officials and beaten up." Atarilal was not alone to experience this. There were a large number of Dhaikar people for whom bamboo work was a traditional occupation.

A similar story was narrated by people of Ghasia community in Joru Khera village (block Dudhi) where the whole community used to make *Kathota* (wood bowl), combs and frames of musical instruments. With the loss of access to forest wood and non-availability of Salai wood, the art is lost. There are 30 families of Ghasia community in this village but no one does wood work any more. They are rendered landless and marginalised.

Photo 6.1: Vasudeo is a blacksmith who cannot do extraction of iron ore due to government policies

Agaria community had the expertise of blacksmithy, extraction of iron ore and smelting it. In the traditional set up there used to be at least one blacksmith in every village who supplied forged iron agriculture implements and kitchen utensils. Mining was done by highly experienced people who knew how to make trenches and mine ore. Typically this work was done in groups of 10 to 12 workers. Extraction was done using coal which was made of *Katha* and *Sakhu* wood.

As mining of iron ore was declared illegal, access to raw material was denied. Vasudeo is a highly skilled blacksmith of Kharahi village but he does not do extraction anymore and makes forged products only. He is worried about accusations police makes on him of theft of ore. The new law of the state converted the one time skilled people into thieves over night.

Sarju Prajapati is 65 years old potter of village Rannu (block Dudhi). The potter family was supported by the village, and it was highly respected. He and his family made earthen items for household usage, and villagers in return gave them grains at the time of harvesting. He recalls that traditionally bride was given five earthen pots. As per the rituals and rites of the tribal people, one potter woman would accompany the bride at the time of marriage. In return they got gifts and alms that supported them well for the entire year.

Photo 6.2: Sarju Prajapati depends on pottery work, in village Rannu (Dudhi block)

The tradition is getting broken. Now Sarju Prajapati sells pots to villagers and in return earns cash or grain. Jajmani system is replaced by capitalist relations. Annually he manages to earn about 10 quintal of grain but the sheen is lost. His son prefers to practice agriculture and take up casual work as a labourer, and is not interested in pottery anymore. Problems are also in plenty. The wood is expensive. The wood that was available for 50 paise per kg is now being sold at Rs. 4 per kg, while the selling price of pots has only marginally gone up. The Gram Sabha land, from where he collected mud, is given out on patta. He finds it difficult to collect mud. The custom of giving pots at the time of marriage appears to be also fading away.

6.2 The Ashram Activities Undertaken for the Revival of Traditional Industry

The work of promotion of crafts sector and building up of village industries was taken up under the Agrindus Project from the beginning. Leaders at the Ashram realised that the sustainability of crafts will depend on the availability of raw materials, skills, and access to market and credit. Therefore, groups of artisans and craftsmen were selected and given training to improve their skills, tools, and raw material. They were also provided credit and marketing channels were opened up to facilitate the sale. Dr. Ragini Prem recalls that when the project started there were no tailors in the villages. Tribals did not know how to stitch clothes and she had to go to city for stitching clothes. Soon tailoring was taken up in the vocational courses in the Ashram schools. The carcasses of animals were being sold at throw away prices, and the Ashram realised that if villagers are taught how to flee and process leather, they will have good quality raw material and surplus leather could be sold in the market outside. Collection, processing and selling of minor forest produce could add substantially to the off season economy. For all these efforts to succeed, people had to be encouraged to use local products made in the village itself. After all, in the Gandhian framework action could not be separated from thought.

Experience showed that there was plenty of scope for developing village industries. As the Ashram took up the integrated development plan of villages, diesel sets were being installed in farms. Technicians were needed to repair pumps and motors. Spinning wheels were installed at homes though the repair of these wheels was done at

Sevagram. There was an immediate need to develop service providers who could provide various technical services. In this way the Ashram worked towards development of khadi and village industries. Various attempts made by the Ashram fell in the following categories:

(1) A number of village technicians were groomed by providing training in repair of diesel engines, auto engines and spinning wheels. This produced pump set mechanics, electricians, and radio mechanics.
(2) Cobblers (*mochi*), blacksmiths (*lohar*), carpenters (*badhai*), masons, potters, rope and bamboo makers were given training. Training was also imparted for collection of bone and hide, and primary processing of leather. Many people were trained in tailoring.
(3) Khadi production was taken up at a large scale. Spinning wheels were distributed. Cotton and silk threads were produced and khadi spinning was encouraged.
(4) Other village level industries that were promoted were bee keeping, production of edible oil, pulse processing, de-husking of rice, spice grinding, soap making, incense sticks, biogas plants, and repair of agriculture implements. The Ashram took up the contracts for collection of minor forest produce, such as *mahua*, *tendu patta* (leaves), *aonla*, *babai* grass and medicinal herbs. They were processed and sold in the local market.

During the period 1960 to 1978, the Ashram carried out intense khadi production activity. Charkhas (spinning wheels) were installed at the Ashram premises, and thousands were distributed to people in villages. In 1979 the Ashram got registration from Khadi and Village Industries Commission (KVIC) and a licence to produce and market cotton, woollen and silk products. The Ashram promoted an improved charkha called Ambar charkha, and started sericulture. Rearing of silk worms began in 1979 on Arjun and Andi trees. This was followed by training of spinners and weavers. By the mid-nineties the production of silk and silk yarn was in full swing.

While the Ashram carried on these activities for more than two decades, the going got tougher with time. Khadi could not face the competition from mill made products and it gradually faced closure. At present khadi spinning and weaving has come to a complete halt. A visit to the marketing outlet in Govindpur shows that there are not many activities that are on any more. The production was viable only till Ashram could pass on subsidy to people. It was also felt that with passing of time it was not easy for a genuine organization to deal with corrupt state institutions and sell khadi with government subsidies as the subsidies will not come easily and timely.

6.3 Training and Empowerment

Photo 6.3: Carpenters working at a workshop in the Ashram premises

As said above, training and skill development has been the thrust area of all the rural development programmes. Workshops were organised, resource persons were invited, exposure trips were arranged and artisans were sent for specialised training programmes outside. Some of the specialised workshops organised were devoted to carpentry, blacksmithy, leathercraft and wood work. In 2011 a few local people were sponsored to attend "Workshop on Agricultural Tools and Blacksmithy" held at Suruchi, Wardha.

In December 2010 the Ashram organised a training programme on the bamboo works. A few master craftsmen from Maharashtra and Assam were invited to be trainers. The local artisans learned about new techniques and got design and product ideas from them. Atri Lal said: "We got art of the bamboo work from our parents. We made baskets and sieve (*soop*). After the training we learned how to make bags, pots, flower vase and dustbins."

Some of the new products were designed to have a high market appeal. They could be sold in the neighbouring town of Renukoot.

Vishwa Kumar is a Chamar (leatherworker) by caste and leather work is his family occupation. When he was young he got associated with the Ashram. His skills were honed through several trainings he received. He remembered going to Varanasi in 1978, as a young man of 22 years, where he received two month long training at Sewapuri. Today he sits at the *Ashram Mode* and earns his livelihood through his family occupation.

Photo 6.4: Vishwa Kumar had received training of leather craft at the Ashram

Jagdishwar lives in Faripan village and is a potter by caste. He reported about several training sessions he attended at the Ashram workshops. He stated that at a later date he was also sent to Bastar for an exposure visit. He learnt many new things that helped him develop new artistic abilities. Today he has a successful product range.

While there are many success stories of training programmes run by the Ashram, with time the enthusiasm for training went down. The Ashram could offer such courses only till the time it had project funding. On their own people did not have the paying capacity to subscribe to such courses, and there are many commercial training centres which do the same work. Presently the vocational courses and training to artisans has come to a near halt.

6.4 Distribution of Identity Cards

Formation of the artisans' union and distribution of identity card (ID) proved to be a major source of empowerment of artisans. The process began in April 2009 and the union was named as 'Karigar Panchayat Sangathan'. Nearly 1,000 artisans became member of this organization. The Sangathan was also linked to the national network of artisans, which gave them a wider exposure. All the members of the Sangathan were issued identity cards by the Ashram. The idea was to unite the artisans and give them strength, dignity and expertise. When artisans joined the union, they also shared their expertise and experiences. So far about 335 identity cards have been issued.

Those who were in the network experienced increased sense of self-confidence. One of them said: "We had lost all respect and were treated as thieves. Now when any official stops us, we show them our ID card and they let us go." Atri Lal Dhaikar (village Khairahi, block Myorepur) makes bamboo products. He says: "My wife and I got the ID card. Now I can show my ID card to forest officials. I am not worried about being blamed about theft." However, the reach of this effort remained very limited. There were many artisans who joined the network with a big hope, but were disappointed when their expectation were not met.

6.5 Providing Raw Materials, Tools and Working Capital

The Ashram, through its various programmes, attempted to provide tools, arrange for raw materials and provide working capital to artisans. Some were also given marketing support by providing visible marketing outlet. Products were also sold through the KVIC outlets. Scarcity of raw materials was a big problem for them and shortage of working capital was an additional challenge. The Ashram identified these bottlenecks and tried to address them. The Ashram has made some efforts to make metal available for blacksmiths. This has been of a limited help, as it helped only a few artisans. However, this was an effort in the right direction.

The Ashram constructed working sheds for 20 weavers. In the year 2009 the Ashram carried out a detailed survey of local artisans.

Photo 6.5: A weaver weaving cotton fabric in Bakuliya Nirman Kendra (Babhni block)

It was estimated that there are nearly 2,200 artisans in the four blocks where the Ashram operates. A plan was made to form 80 Self Help Groups (SHGs) of artisans so that raw material, tools and skills could be rendered easily. So far only 5 SHGs have been formed and only one has been linked to bank.

6.6 Impact of Programmes of Rural Industrialization

The handicraft sector is facing several challenges. Handcraft products produced in the villages are losing in competition with machine made items. Nevertheless, due to the efforts of the Ashram some of the traditional arts and crafts of the villages are able to survive. Ideology has certainly been a major substratum of whatever little success has been attained in this field.

6.7 Survival of Traditional Crafts

In the race for modernity young people are quitting their traditional work. Better remuneration lures them to areas other than craftwork. Yet, in the villages where the Ashram has worked, villagers are still continuing with their tradition. In the blocks where the Ashram has its presence, about two-third of all the respondents reported pursuing their traditional occupation. It is noticeable that the percentage of those pursuing the traditional occupation is significantly higher in the area where the Ashram has worked as compared to the areas where the Ashram has not worked (Table 6.1).

Table 6.1: Families in which Traditional Occupations are Still Being Pursued

Occupational Status	*Ashram blocks*		*Non Ashram blocks*		*Total*	
	No.	*%*	*No.*	*%*	*No.*	*%*
Pursuing it*	546	64.31	88	51.46	634	62.16
Not pursuing it*	303	35.69	83	48.54	386	37.84
Total	**849**	**100.00**	**171**	**100.00**	**1020**	**100.00**

* The difference between the Ashram and the Non-ashram blocks is significant at 5 per cent level of significance.

An analysis was carried out for prominent crafts to see percentage of people who had a traditional craft and are still pursuing it. A comparison of the Ashram and the non-Ashram blocks shows that a higher percentage of artisans are pursuing the traditional craft in the Ashram villages (Table 6.2) as compared to the non-Ashram villages. This difference may be attributed to the Ashram's efforts that empowered them and gave them the ability to make products

Table 6.2: Per cent Artisans who are Pursuing Traditional Craft

Occupation	*Ashram blocks*		*Non-Ashram blocks*		*Total*	
	No.	*%*	*No.*	*%*	*No.*	*%*
Collecting herbs*	384	68.33	11	34.38	395	66.50
Blacksmithy (*Lohar*)*	53	65.43	4	22.22	57	57.58
Carpentery (*Badhai*)	6	31.58	4	17.39	10	23.81
Pottery (*Kumhar*)	8	72.73	31	88.57	39	84.78
Barbery (*Nai*)	12	100.00	5	62.50	17	85.00

* The difference between the Ashram and the Non-ashram blocks is significant at 5 per cent level of significance.

to suit changing preferences of people. It has also given them a sense of pride. The Ashram's work with blacksmiths shows good results as still a large number of them in the Ashram villages pursue blacksmithy.

6.8 Improved Skills

Table 6.3 below shows the extent of concentration of artisans, technicians and service providers in the Ashram and the non-Ashram villages. The artisans are typically more in the Ashram villages compared to the non-Ashram villages. And this is true for all the types of arts and crafts included in the study except weavers. There is a large difference in the number of drivers and motor mechanics between the two areas. The role of the Ashram in developing a cadre of electricians, technicians, drivers and mechanics cannot be overestimated although to some extent these differences may also arise from the fact of the larger concentration of tribal population in the Ashram villages without access to enough cultivable land.

Table 6.3: Artisans, Technicians and Service Providers in Survey Villages

(Number per village)

Occupational category	*Ashram blocks*	*Non-Ashram blocks*	*Total*
Barber	1.80	0.50	1.48
Blacksmith	2.57	0.20	1.98
Carpenter	8.17	4.70	7.30
Cobbler	4.63	0.90	3.70
Driver	19.97	6.00	16.48
Electrician	2.10	0.10	1.60
Motor mechanic	11.07	3.40	9.15
Potter	2.67	1.10	2.27
Tailor	0.43	0.20	0.38
Veterinary specialist	0.37	0.10	0.30
Washerman	6.53	0.50	5.03
Weaver	0.03	0.80	0.23

6.9 Survival of Local Dance and Music

The Ashram laid such a strong emphasis on local art and culture that it is clearly visible amongst all those who are associated with their programmes—be it their volunteers, teachers or students. One teacher stated: "Our children enjoy playing local music and perform the traditional dances. Children of other schools have switched to Bollywood songs." This claim is not at all unfounded. *Domkatch*, *Karma* and *Shalla* dance forms are still very popular, and more so in the Ashram villages. Table 6.4 shows that a significantly larger percentage of parents residing in the Ashram area reported that their children knew local art forms than those in the non-Ashram areas. This again could also be due to larger percentage of tribal population in the Ashram area. As compared to others, the tribals are still more known for their interest in culture and traditions which is closely boundup with their identity.

Table 6.4: Percentage of Respondents Who said that their Children Perform/Know Traditional Songs and Dances

Do your children know local dances and sing local songs	*Ashram blocks*		*Non-Ashram blocks*		*Total*	
	No.	*%*	*No.*	*%*	*No.*	*%*
Yes	233	62.35	42	20.90	275	34.20
No	370	37.48	159	79.10	529	65.20

★ The difference between Ashram and Non-ashram blocks is significant at 5 per cent level of significance.

6.10 Conclusion

In sum, the Ashram has undertaken several steps to revive village industry. They include training, demonstration, mobilization and provision of resources. Forming network of artisans and providing them with ID cards was done to give them self-confidence, empower them and provide them some dignity. However, this effort could not seek the scale it was meant to be, and remained limited to only a few artisans. The major problem comes from the declining demand for the produce of village arts and crafts. This confirms the Gandhian view that the economic issues cannot be separated from the value system of society. Experience has shown that it is difficult for the village industry to compete with modern industry. The Ashram attempted to present a model of development and justice that will remain alive to provide a critique of modernization, albeit it could not pass the test of sustainability.

CHAPTER 7

Health

At the time the Ashram was established in Sonbhadra, health facilities in the project area were almost non-existent. Malnutrition, hunger, diseases and unhealthy living conditions were characteristics of the local population. People were commonly suffering from tropical diseases like malaria, diarrhoea, tuberculosis, skin diseases and sexually transmitted diseases. At the same time, as some respondents stated, those who lived in forests and could follow traditional practices, had better health than those who suffered from forced settlement or were living in marginal environment. The latter were a greater victim of illnesses and destitution. The availability of forest resources decreased rapidly due to loss of forest and freedom to access them. To certain extent the high morbidity and poor health conditions showed that there was a disruption in the tradition that they followed for centuries. Minor forest produce, like *chironjee* and *aonla*, which formed part of their regular diet once, had gradually disappeared, reportedly due to environmental pollution. Much of their indigenous knowledge base of herbs stood redundant due to disappearance of required herbs and plants.

7.1 Approach

The Ashram took a holistic view on health with the goal of making people self-reliant in primary health care. Initially, the Ashram gave priority to developing more health awareness among the local people. Based on Gandhian philosophy, the Ashram's programmes were heavily focused on empowering communities so that they could take care of their health related needs themselves. An understanding of the prevalent diseases and their prevention was central to this programme. People were informed about nutrition, health, sanitation and need to clean up their drinking water sources. They were motivated to accept small family norms and planned parenthood. Home remedies were popularised and cultivation of herbs that were traditionally used for medicinal value was encouraged. Setting up of *Ghar Bagia* (kitchen garden) was taken up on a large scale. A cadre of health workers was created and local *dais* (birth attendants) were given training in healthy parturition practices. These health workers formed an important link between the Ashram and the people.

Ashram's approach for safe deliveries was not to take mothers to health facilities but to create effective network of *dais*. Training of *dais* in the safe delivery methods and hygiene was taken up to ensure that the health care is available at home and the critical cases can be referred to the nearby facilities when required. As a matter of preference home deliveries were promoted over institutional delivery by both people and the Ashram. This was done more for practical reasons, as the health facilities were not easily accessible and the quality of services was much below the desired level.

The Ashram promoted minimum use of medicines for treatment. In the process the Ashram accepted many indigenous practices, the healthy traditions and practices prevalent in the villages for long. It has not opposed the traditional cultural practice of breastfeeding and early introduction of supplementary food when the climate seemed to be against this. But it dismissed *tantra*, magical beliefs, and superstitions which were considered to be irrational. The rejection of *tantric* practices was done also because it was rooted in personal animosity, jealousy and prejudices. While the Ashram instilled confidence among people in their traditional practices, it vociferously fought against superstitions and evil practices. Its approach was to focus on inspiring and empowering people to act in the interest of health promotion. It abstained from assuming permanent responsibility of people's health.

7.2 The Activities

A clinic was set up in the Ashram Campus and was run by Dr. Ragini Prem herself. Other activities were awareness generation amongst villagers and training camps. Looking at the shortage of health manpower in the area, the Ashram invited the villagers and started training them. Under the Agrindus project the Ashram took up health programme in 1968 to raise awareness amongst people and empower them to take care of their health. The Ashram was conducting various health awareness activities in the project area. The goal was to make people self-reliant in health rather than assuming permanent responsibility for people's health. Moreover, since 1975 it took up as a more structured health intervention programme under which a new institutional set up was created. Between 1975 and 1980 health workers were trained for recognizing and treating common ailments and referring serious cases to appropriate health facility. *Dais* were also trained in safe delivery practices. Since 1990 Gram Sakhis, village level volunteers, have been inducted as health friends. Their role is to spread awareness amongst rural women on the issues of mother and child care. Annual Health Campaign (AHC), also known as Swastha Raksha Abhiyan is to build health awareness about seasonal diseases. Bleaching powder is made available in villages for chlorination of drinking water sources in rainy season.

Some efforts were also made to strengthen health manpower at the village level. As part of this policy, the Ashram's health interventions were executed at three levels. At the village level Swastha Mitras were placed for awareness generation and referrals. At the cluster level there were Nirman Kendras where Village Doctors or Arogya Mitras were placed. At this level health facilities were set up for primary health care. At the district level Health Education and Training Centre, also referred as Arogya Kendra, was set up by Dr. Ragini Prem herself. Patients with ailments and delivery cases are handled here. Cases with complications are sent to specialised hospitals for referrals.

During 1979-80 when a number of Nirman Kendras were established, the Ashram also provided a Swastha Mitra for each Nirman Kendra. By the year 2002 there were 10 health facilities with 12 village doctors who took care of clinical problems. In addition, each village was given a Swastha Mitra whose róle was to create health awareness, and telling people about preventive measures against the dominant diseases. The Ashram promoted the traditional practices such as use of turmeric and *gur*, and encouraged people to do turmeric cultivation. As mentioned earlier, in those days there was a rampant belief in magic and witchcraft and people who were believed to have been affected by evil spirits were beaten and insulted. The Ashram made a serious attempt to curb this practice.

Since 1990 the health programme was expanded to include Gram Sakhis (women Swastha Mitras). Gram Sakhis were given rigorous health training so that they could spread health awareness amongst rural women. In 2008-09 Swastha Raksha Abhiyan was launched with the help of Swastha Mitras and Gram Sakhis, during which use of clean drinking water, preventive measures, nutrition and home remedies were popularised.

Major health activities of the Ashram cover the following:

(1) Annual Health Campaigns (AHCs) are organised every year with the help of Gram Sakhis and Swastha Mitras and are still the pivotal component of the health programmes of the Ashram. This is held before the onset of the monsoon so that people are reminded of necessary precautions to take for malaria, diarrhoea and skin allergies.
(2) Close to 4,000 drinking water sources have been cleaned up during the campaigns.
(3) Gram Sakhis have been conducting health awareness among women in the villages.
(4) Traditional *dais* (birth attendants) for home deliveries have been trained by the Ashram. In particular, *dais* were told to use sterilized new blade and sterilized thread for cutting and tying umbilical cord. Dais are informed about delivery and post delivery complications during as well as timely referrals. Infants care and spacing child birth are part of their agenda.
(5) The Ashram has promoted the concept of *Ghar Bagia* and cultivation of medicinal herbs. Use of aonla, *lemon grass*,

zeera, *gurich ka kada*, turmeric and other local herbs was encouraged. Ashram's packets of *panch fons* (five powders) were quite popular among people for common ailments.

(6) Health camps have been organised quite frequently for eye tests and health check ups. Eye camps were also quite successful where hundreds of villagers could get cataract operations. For these activities the Ashram worked in close association with the doctors of public health system and those of private hospitals.

(7) The Ashram conducted health check ups in the schools. More than 7,000 children were benefited.

(8) Printing of literature and health exhibits for use by health workers and villagers.

(9) Each year approximately 18,000 cases are handled at the Arogya Kendra in campus and 6000 cases are handled at other 4 health centres.

7.3 Concept of Health

The study explored the tribal concept of health and illness, as it has a direct implication on their health seeking behaviour. The tribal concept of health is a perspective that is anchored in people's traditional beliefs, practices and their interactions with the physical environment around them. The people of Sonbhadra carried a long tradition of herbal medicines and health care. They, like tribals in other places, were faced with modernity and found it difficult to cope with the multitude of changes around them. The depletion of forest cover and people's reduced access to forests made food intake difficult, leading to nutritional deficiency. Tribals also lost access to medicinal herbs that grew in forests. All this has an impact on the way the tribal people think of health and illness. People's concepts of good health are shown in the Box 7.1.

For most of the people, health is physical, whereby a person is considered to be healthy if all ten of his organs are functioning well and he or she looks charming, and hale and hearty. For some people it is also the ability of the person to carry out physical activities and earn his or her livelihood. To quote a typical respondent "A person who can carry out normal activities of life without getting fatigue.

BOX 7.1: CONCEPT OF GOOD HEALTH

1. A person is healthy if he can labour, do his own work, and toil without getting tired.
2. A healthy person has a healthy face, looks fresh all the time, has attractive looks and has bright appearance.
3. A person who is disease free is in a good health.
4. When a person has a good appetite, it means his health is good.
5. Healthy people have a sharp mind, are alert and have quick responses.
6. When a person breaths well without interruption, it is a sign of good health.
7. A person with regular routine like getting up early, going to toilet, and working in the field is surely healthy.
8. A person in good health is tension free; he smiles and looks relaxed.

Walking 10 to 15 km, toiling in the fields should not tire him." Good health is reflected through healthy appetite, sound sleep, regularity of routine and a bright face. For some, good health is synonymous with stress free and relaxed condition.

7.4 Drinking Water and Sanitation

Drinking water quality is a critical issue in Sonbhadra. According to official sources many of the illnesses among people are due to lack of clean drinking water. People are affected by waterborne diseases and children often suffer from diarrhoea. Analysis of data collected through the primary survey of adults reveals that nearly 45 per cent respondents reported that clean drinking water is not available to them throughout the year (Table 7.1). (The concept of clean drinking water was subjective, however. The respondents judged for themselves whether the drinking water available to them was clean or not.) Similar response is obtained from Sarpanchs. Out of 40 survey villages 19 villages reported non-availability of clean drinking water throughout the year. During the summer time the wells dry up and people succumb to use water from all types of unsafe sources. In Padri village (Myorepur block) situation became so critical in the last summer that several people and animals died after drinking water from the dam. The problem seems to be equally acute in both the Ashram area and outside.

Table 7.1: Availability of Good Quality Drinking Water

Availability of good quality water throughout the year	*Ashram villages*		*Non-Ashram villages*		*Total*	
	No.	*%*	*No.*	*%*	*No.*	*%*
N	603		201		804	
Available	332	55.06	116	57.71	448	55.72
Not-available	271	44.94	85	42.29	356	44.28
Source: Adult schedule						
N	30		10		40	
Available	15	50.00	6	60.00	21	52.50
not available	15	50.00	4	40.00	19	47.50

Source: Sarpanch schedule.

Photo 7.1: Young girls carrying water from outside the village

As a matter of fact it is not the Ashram area and outside (covered in this study) only but the entire district of Sonbhadra suffers from the problem of shortage of drinking water. In some areas the water table has dipped so low that the hand pumps and tube wells are failing. This problem is worse in Babhni and Dudhi blocks. Groundwater too has become polluted due to heavy concentration of industries in Chopan and Myorepur blocks. Out of 40 Sarpanchs 21 reported that the underground water is polluted.

In and around the Singrauli area, the region considered to be largest industrial area of Asia due to concentration of power plants, is affected by fluoride. Atmospheric deposition of fluoride-containing emissions from coal-fired power plants and other industrial sources also contributes to presence of pollutants beyond permissible amounts. This is caused, either by direct deposition or by deposition to soil and subsequent runoff of chemicals.

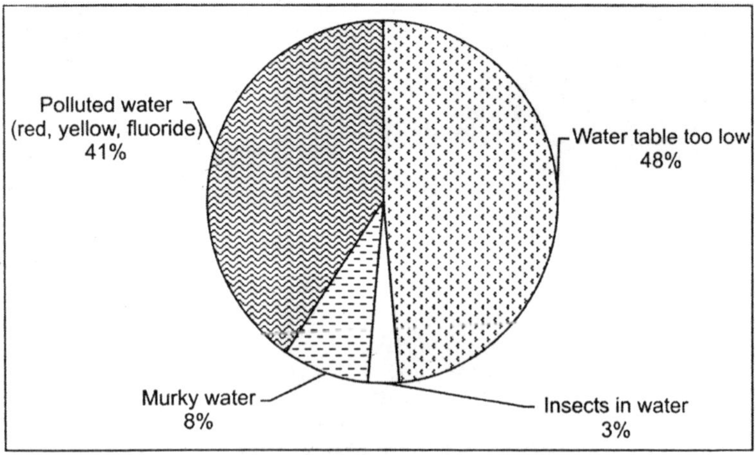

Fig. 7.1: Nature of problems

7.5 Living the Old Tradition

Some of the community practices started by the Ashram are still alive in villages. One such thing is that villagers maintained their drinking water sources well and kept them clean. In village Paraspani (Dudhi block) the handpump on which nearly 15 families were dependent, stopped working. They complained to the Sarpanch,

Photo 7.2: Water from a clean well

but hand pump was not repaired. They filed their complaint at the BDO office, but nobody listened to them and the hand pump remained out of order. Munna Lal decided to overcome the obstacle and he collected other young people of the neighbourhood. Soon he had Jagdish, Bhagwan Das and Hira Lal with him. They were tired of getting the hand pump fixed every now and then. They thought of rehabilitating old well of the village. The water of this well was unusable because it was full of rotten leaves and filth. They decided to clean it up. It took them more than a week but at the end fifteen families and their animals started getting clean drinking water.

The practice of putting chlorine in drinking water sources by villagers and Ashram workers is also visible in most of the Ashram villages. Akamaniya Devi, Sakhi of Bairpur village (Chopan block) said: "Last year after the rains stopped, I myself put bleaching powder in twenty five wells of different clusters of villages."

7.6 Sanitation

People are not in the habit of constructing and using household level toilets. This is not unusual, however. In much of the rural India, even in socio-economically developed regions open defecation is a reality. People prefer to go to forest area, fields or roads for defecation. In many houses toilets have been constructed under Total Sanitation Campaign (TSC) and Indira Awas Yojana (IAY). However, their usage is minimal. As shown by Table 7.2, 96.68 per cent respondents in the Ashram area reported going for open defecation. The percentage of those going for open defecation in the Ashram area is significantly lower than in the area outside the Ashram activities.

Table 7.2: Toilets

Usage of toilet	*Ashram villages*		*Non Ashram villages*		*Total*	
	No.	*%*	*No.*	*%*	*No.*	*%*
N	603		201		804	
Private toilet	16	2.65	1	0.50	17	2.11
Group toilet	1	0.17	0	0.00	1	0.12
Community toilet	3	0.50	0	0.00	3	0.37
Open defecation *	583	96.68	200	99.50	783	97.39

* The difference between the Ashram and the Non-ashram blocks is significant at 5 per cent level of significance.

7.7 Personal Hygiene

Table 7.3 shows the extent of hygiene practices. It is evident from the table that only two in three respondents handle drinking water properly. Only half of the respondents reported brushing teeth regularly and most of them used *datoon* (neem stick). There is no difference between the Ashram area and outside. Yet, the researchers observed that Ashram villages were much cleaner than the non Ashram villages. Their children appeared neater and the houses were also kept cleaner.

Table 7.3: Hygiene Practices

Hygiene practices	*Ashram villages*		*Non-Ashram villages*		*Total*	
	No.	*%*	*No.*	*%*	*No.*	*%*
N	603		201		804	
Drinking water is handled properly	401	66.50	132	65.67	533	66.29
Teeth are brushed regularly	596	98.84	199	99.00	795	98.88
with *datoon**	541	90.02	165	82.50	706	88.14
with brush & tooth paste	38	6.32	13	6.50	51	6.37
with tooth powder	20	3.33	22	11.00	42	5.24
with other things	2	0.33	0	0.00	2	0.25
Total responses	601		200		801	

* The difference between Ashram and Non-ashram blocks is significant at 5 per cent level of significance.

Source: Adult Schedule.

7.8 Balanced Diet

The Ashram worked to popularise things which were locally available, and had high nutritional value. Dr. Ragini Prem recalls: "I told people to consume *til* (sesame) during winter months. It was a good safeguard against flurosis". People were taught how to make *ladoos of methi* (fenugreek seeds), *ladoos of mahua* and roasted *til*. It was there in the tradition to give *gur*-turmeric mixture to women for several days after their delivery. The Ashram's efforts rejuvenated faith of people in their own system and taught them about balanced diet. Cultivation of turmeric and *til* was popularised in the region. The Ashram told people not to sell *arhar* (pulses) and keep it for their own use. Some of these practices are still quite popular in the Ashram villages. The findings of the survey on the availability of balanced diet are shown below. Table 7.4 shows that less than half of the respondents only are able to have *dal* as part of their meals. Less than a quarter of respondents get vegetables and only one in ten gets milk. As compared to the villages outside the Ashram area, the Ashram villages seem to have a greater consumption of *dal* but they have lesser access to milk, perhaps due to lesser number of buffaloes per capita (Chapter 5).

Table 7.4: Availability of Balanced Diet

Type of diet	Ashram villages		Non Ashram villages		Total	
	No.	%	No.	%	No.	%
N	603		201		804	
Roti & rice	591	98.01	195	97.01	786	97.76
Dal (lentil)	280	46.43	76	37.81	356	44.28
Green vegetables	143	23.71	47	23.38	190	23.63
Milk	60	9.95	38	18.91	98	12.19

Source: Adult Schedule

7.9 Institutional Deliveries

Home deliveries are the preferred choice of people in the Ashram villages (Table 7.5). The percentage of those who prefer home delivery is significantly higher in the Ashram villages (77.61%) as compared to the non-Ashram villages (51.2%). In the non-Ashram villages close to one in four respondents prefers a Primary Health Centre (PHC). Percentages of those preferring Community Health Centre (CHC), district hospital and private hospital are also higher in the non-Ashram villages. It was recorded that the per cent of institutional deliveries in the district is much lower than the national average.

Table 7.5: Preferred Place of Delivery

Preferred place of delivery	Ashram villages		Non-Ashram villages		Total	
	No.	%	No.	%	No.	%
Home*	468	77.61	103	51.2	571	71.0
PHC*	50	8.29	47	23.4	97	12.1
CHC	8	1.33	9	4.5	17	2.1
District Hospital	2	0.33	6	3.0	8	1.0
Private Hospital	8	1.33	11	5.5	19	2.4
Other	65	10.78	24	11.9	89	11.1

* The difference between Ashram and Non-ashram blocks is significant at 5 per cent level of significance.

Source: Adult Schedule.

However when the question was put up to the new mothers who had delivered in the last six months, the findings were different.

Out of 141 mothers who answered the question the occurrence of home deliveries in the Ashram villages was 54.33 per cent and in the non-Ashram villages was 31.42 per cent. This shows that the trend to move to hospital is catching up with government schemes in place and more so because of Janani Suraksha Yojana (JSY) but Ashram still believes that for most women it is not practical to utilise the institutional set up of government, and therefore, home deliveries with skilled *dais* is still a better option for the villagers. Although this is beyond the scope of the study but it may be mentioned that the respondents have commonly expressed deep sense of dissatisfaction with the actual working of JSY. There were complaints about cuts, inessential referrals to outside specialists, lack of facilities at the PHC/CHC and a lack of sensitivity and concern on the part of providers.

It is, therefore, not a surprise to see that the ante-natal check up (ANC) was reported by only 16.43 per cent mothers of the Ashram villages, who had delivered in the last six months, as compared to 28.57 per cent in the non-Ashram villages. The difference may also be more due to a lower socio-economic condition and remoteness of village under the Ashram projects.

7.10 Major Health Problems in the Region

Malaria, diarrhoea, skin disorders and tuberculosis (TB) appear to be the most common ailments prevalent in this region. According to the respondents (Adult Schedule) the most common problems are cough and cold, malaria, tuberculosis, skin problems, jaundice and typhoid. The Infant Mortality Rate (IMR) of the district stands at 77 per 1,000 births (Annual Health Survey 2010-11) and the district Sonbhadra is far from the MDG 4 goal to achieve the target of 28 per 1,000 births by the year 2015.

According to the official figures Sonbhadra district has a much higher malaria burden. The malaria annual parasite index stands at 19.2, which is quite high. Malaria is commonly found in almost all villages. Nearly 10 per cent of the respondents said that at least one of their family members suffered from malaria during the last one year. The actual incidence may be higher due to non-detection of cases. There is no significant difference in the incidence of malaria in the Ashram and the non-Ashram-villages. In the Ashram villages where use of mosquito net was popularised, one does not see these nets any more. People create smoke of neem leaves to deal with mosquito menace.

The TB patients are there in almost all villages and there is stigma attached to it. Often there are cases of snake and scorpion bites in the villages. People go to faith healer or *Vish Vaidya* for such problems. Other health problems mentioned during the discussion included cough and cold. The common treatment mentioned for this problem was taking home remedies such as *gur*, honey, and crushed *tulsi* leaves. Diarrhoea is another common problem especially among young children.

To gauge the trend in pattern of morbidity, health workers were interviewed. The category of health workers interviewed were Accredited Social Health Activists (ASHAs), village *dais*, traditional healers, doctors, and Swastha Mitras and *dais* of the Ashram. Their responses are shown in Table 7.6 below. It appears that there is a

Table 7.6: Trends of Major Diseases

Trends in the occurrences of diseases	*Ashram Villages*		*Non-Ashram Villages*		*Total*	
	No.	*%*	*No.*	*%*	*No.*	*%*
Health Worker Schedule	47		8		55	
Malaria						
Increasing	23	48.94	4	50.00	27	49.09
Same as before	1	2.13	2	25.00	3	5.45
Decreasing	23	48.94	2	25.00	25	45.45
Can't say	0	0.00	0	0.00	0	0.00
Diarrhoea						
Increasing	11	23.40	4	50.00	15	27.27
Same as before	10	21.28	2	25.00	12	21.82
Decreasing	26	55.32	2	25.00	28	50.91
Can't say	0	0.00	0	0.00	0	0.00
Tuberculosis						
Increasing	13	27.66	1	12.50	14	25.45
Same as before	7	14.89	3	37.50	10	18.18
Decreasing	25	53.19	4	50.00	29	52.73
Can't say	2	4.26	0	0.00	2	3.64
Skin Disorders						
Increasing	14	29.79	3	37.50	17	30.91
Same as before	6	12.77	1	12.50	7	12.73
Decreasing	24	51.06	4	50.00	28	50.91
Can't say	3	6.38	0	0.00	3	5.45

somewhat increasing trend in prevalence of malaria, and a somewhat decreasing trend in prevalence of diarrhoea, tuberculosis and skin disorders.

7.11 Health Seeking Behaviour

Respondents were asked about what they do when it comes to seeking treatment. Table 7.7 shows the first line of treatment, as reported by the respondents while canvassing the adult schedule. By far it is the *Jhola Chaap* doctors (quacks) whom people trust the most. Each village has one or more *Jhola Chaap* doctors, called Bengali doctors, who are quite popular. They typically go around on motor cycle moving home to home. *Jhola Chaap* doctors are not certified medical practitioners and yet they have the biggest hold on people. Villagers have good faith on *Jhola Chaap* doctors. According to Manoj Kumar, a ward member of Manbasa village (Dudhi block) "*Jhola Chaap* doctors are the only hope of the people". They serve them when sickness strikes. Professionally trained doctors are so expensive that villagers cannot afford. A quack is most easily available. Convenience and cost also play an important role in their decision to contact a quack for treatment. We call them quacks but they are inseparably linked with the collective consciousness of the community. They play an important role in

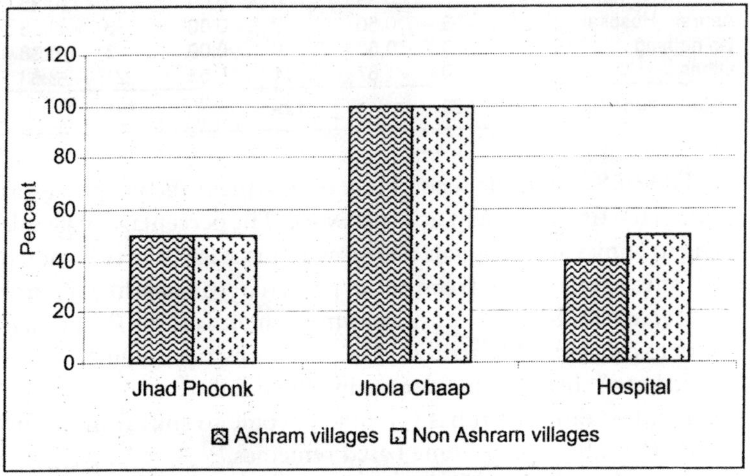

Fig. 7.2: Frequency of choices people make (1st or 2nd choice)

the integration of tribal society. In Sonbhadra district most of the *Jhola Chaap* doctors claim to have procured a recognizable medical degree from some obscure place in Bengal or some other places. One may argue that in the changing circumstances the need is to provide them (the quacks) with scientific understanding of diseases and remedies and not to confront them. The Ashram has worked towards raising awareness among both villagers and the traditional healers, accepting their useful practices and disapproving their misrepresentations. This may explain why the proportion of those going to quacks in the Ashram villages is not much below the same in the non-Ashram villages.

Table 7.7: Frequencies of 1st Line of Treatment

1st line of treatment	*Ashram villages*		*Non-Ashram villages*		*Total*	
	No.	*%*	*No.*	*%*	*No.*	*%*
N	603		201		804	
Home remedy	42	7.00	0	0.00	42	5.26
Jadoo Tona	53	8.83	15	7.54	68	8.51
Jhola Chaap doctor	415	69.17	146	73.37	561	70.21
PHC	34	5.67	7	3.52	41	5.13
CHC	9	1.50	3	1.51	12	1.50
Private hospital or clinic	26	4.33	15	7.54	41	5.13
Ashram Swastha Mitra	3	0.50	2	1.01	5	0.63
Ashram Nirman Kendra	2	0.33	0	0.00	2	0.25
Ashram Hospital	3	0.50	0	0.00	3	0.38
Do nothing	3	0.50	0	0.00	3	0.38
Other	10	1.67	11	5.53	21	2.63
Total responses	**600**		**199**		**799**	

Table 7.8 shows the second line of treatment the people resort to when the first treatment does not work. The percentage of people going to clinics and hospitals increases at this stage. It may be noted that the movement from one practice to another is not unidirectional. While in most cases movement is from *Jhola Chaap* doctor to proper health facility (PHC, CHC, district hospital, private hospital etc.) there are incidences in which failure to get effective treatment or discomfort has prompted people to shift from health facility to traditional or home based remedies.

It may be noted that in the past in Sonbhadra area, as elsewhere,

Table 7.8: Frequencies of 2nd Line of Treatment

2nd line of treatment	*Ashram villages*		*Non-Ashram villages*		*Total*	
	No.	*%*	*No.*	*%*	*No.*	*%*
N	603		201		804	
Home remedy	3	0.50	0	0.00	3	0.37
Jadoo Tona	38	6.44	14	7.04	52	6.59
Jhola Chaap doctor	84	14.24	47	23.62	131	16.60
PHC*	168	28.47	12	6.03	180	22.81
CHC	81	13.73	13	6.53	94	11.91
District Hospital*	19	3.22	108	54.27	127	16.10
Private hospital or clinic*	177	30.00	3	1.51	180	22.81
Ashram Swastha Mitra	5	0.85	0	0.00	5	0.63
Ashram Nirman Kendra	2	0.34	0	0.00	2	0.25
Do nothing	2	0.34	1	0.50	3	0.38
Other	11	1.86	1	0.50	12	1.52
Total responses	**590**		**199**		**789**	

rural folk believed that cure of ailments exist in nature and that there are super natural forces behind illness. For them the village healer is in possession of both the knowledge of the physical world and metaphysical powers. Tribal people followed traditional health practices and the medicine men of the village would do *jhad phoonk* (magic). They (magic men) collected herbs, gave medical advice and performed supernatural treatments such as spells, gave amulets to ward off evil spirits and performed magical practices.

There are thousands of healers in Sonbhadra district who placate the deities and intimidate evil spirits. Magic and traditional herbal remedies are all mixed up. Almost everyone is familiar with the local herbs and their medicinal properties. Use of these herbal recipes for common problems is a normal practice. When the problem persists or the ailment is more serious, they go to healers for appeasing the spirits. When the healer doing *jhad phoonk* suggests that the bad spirits have been tackled, and recommends that the patient should be examined by a doctor, patients are taken to doctors.

Table 7.9 shows the availability of traditional healers. There are a large number of healers in the area and clearly their concentration is much higher in the Ashram villages because the traditional practices continue to be in vogue. The traditional art of healing has been passed on from a Guru to his disciples. People chosen by *Guru*

Table 7.9: Traditional Healers in Ashram and non-Ashram Villages

Type of healers	*Ashram villages*		*Non-Ashram villages*		*Total*	
	No.	*Average per village*	*No.*	*Average per village*	*No.*	*Average per village*
N	30		10		40	
Herbal healers	113	3.76	8	0.80	121	3.02
Vish Vaisya (snake and scorpion bites)	208	6.93	34	3.40	242	6.05
Healers for jhad-phoonk, Tantra, Magical practices	165	5.50	52	5.20	217	5.42
Bone Setters	47	1.56	22	2.20	69	1.72
Special healers	6	0.20	1	0.10	7	0.17

to give *vidya* assemble on a full moon night in the month of *Sawan* (July). Each one is given a pole which is believed to be having a special power. The *Guru* teaches about herbs and demonstrates black magic. At the end they all sing and dance together. Slowly the disciples pick up the healing by assisting the *Guru* and meditating to purify their own mind and body. The patients offer them animals for sacrifice. However, they are not completely dependent on magic for their survival; they also do agricultural works. They do not charge for their services but people get them goats and chickens along with liquor for performing sacrifice.

The traditional healers also work in specialised areas like treatment of eye diseases, poisons (snake and insect bites), bone setting and so on. Tribals believe in *mantras* and in their divine power. Ram Prasad, who learnt *jhad phoonk* from his Guru in Padrach (Chopan block) says: "We have a six line *mantra*. When we start chanting *mantra*, body of the person who had snakebite begins to twist. Slowly the blue tinge of the body begins to disappear and very soon person recovers fully." He tells that to make medicine for scorpion bite, we catch scorpion on Tuesday or Saturday, and put it in a bottle filled with kerosene oil. This is kept for about 21 days. Then the oil is filtered and applied at the place scorpion has stung. Reportedly, the effect of poison goes down immediately. In case this medicine is not available, a local herb called Reni is used. The roots of this herb are put in the mouth of the person affected by scorpion bite. Liquor made of Mahua is also used as a herbal medicine to ooze poison out of the body of the affected person. The Ashram has a non-dualist stand on traditional medicine. It always believed that there is a need to study long living experiential traditions and learn from them low cost, locally available and effective processes while fighting the superstitions, and not completely rejecting the modern medicine.

Certain illnesses are specially thought to have been generated from supernatural causes, for which getting *jhad phoonk* was essential. When someone falls sick the first thing people suspect is that the patient is affected by evil spirits and then *jhad phoonk* should be done to take care. To quote Rajan: "*okhai ke sab kasht door ho jat hai aur ala bala door ho jat hai*" (from this only all sufferings end and evil spirits are far removed). Some situations in which magic is resorted to are shown in the boxes (Photo 7.3).

The faith healers are supposed to act religiously and impartially. "If anyone is bitten by a snake, we are called. We have to leave all other work and rush immediately to help". According to a faith healer "depending on the level of poison we decide on the herb to be used". Also they are not supposed to use their knowledge for creating any friction in the community.

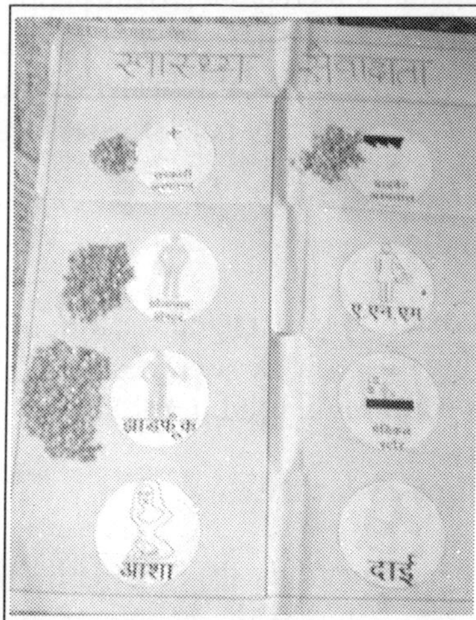

- Kapar dukhat (headache and dizziness)
- *Hawa pani lag gai* (affected by evil spirit)
- *Ghama loo me ghoomat hai* (woman was roaming out in heat waves on a hot summer day)
- *Pila pad gaya* (jaundice)
- Snake bite or scorpion bite
- *Ulti dast* (child affected by *nazar* or evil eye leading to loose motions and vomiting)
- *Garbh bandhwana (*tie sanctified thread to protect womb)

Photo 7.3: Health facilities

60 years old Amarjeet of Jarha village (Myorepur block) is an alumnus of the Ashram school. He himself is a faith healer. People come to him when affected by spirits. He also treats people for snake and scorpion bites, piles, jaundice and STI. Pregnant women come for his blessings so that their pregnancy is safe. He uses a combination of herbs and *mantras* to bless the pregnant woman. He gives a *tabeez* to wear in a chain and is able to examine pulse of patients. He starts *pooja* (to placate gods) by pleasing 40 *devtas* (gods) before ghosts are shoed away. This art came to him from his ancestors. There are special techniques to handle abortions. *Kokh Sajji* (abortion) is also performed by healers.

Situation is changing gradually. People know that going to quacks has at times harmed the people. It increased their suffering and in some cases even caused death. One is not always safe in the hands of *Jhola Chaap* doctors. Urmila, a seventeen year old girl from village Chatarpur (Dudhi block) lost her mother a year back because of treatment from a *Jhola Chaap* doctor. She told that her mother was suffering from high fever. She was taken to a *Jhola Chaap* doctor of the village, who charged Rs. 100 for giving her an injection. She was also given saline water. Her condition worsened overnight and she passed away in the morning of the third day. But since the alternatives are also not easy, dependable and effective, so the people continue to depend on quacks and traditional healers. From a certain perspective continuing dependence of people on faith healers is the indicator of failure of the modern health system to reach the remote and tribal areas.

7.12 Applications of Home Remedies

During this study an attempt was made to understand what home remedies people normally use during various types of illnesses. Box 7.2 lists the major home remedies commonly used in the region.

7.13 Awareness and Misconceptions about Diseases

Despite the Ashram's awareness programmes the villages suffer from low level of awareness about diseases. Among the people of this region, there are several misconceptions about the common diseases

BOX 7.2: POPULAR HOME REMEDIES

- *Kadha* (concoction) of *tulsi*, ginger and honey for cough and cold.
- Roots of *pehta* for stomach problem.
- Turmeric and *gur* paste to women soon after delivery.
- Semar root with water for protection from cough and cold.
- Paste of *jau* flour on persons affected by heat.
- *Lakda* juice for stomach ache.
- Paste of *sindoor* on head for protection from loo (heatwaves).
- Juice of *tulsi* leaves with lemon for malaria.
- Paste of bark of *jamun* tree to control loose motions.
- *Gonjal* roots for fever of any type.
- Lime mixed with *khair* leaves on open wounds.
- Bark of *karam* with black pepper for malaria.
- Drink prepared from *hadjod* for malaria and its paste for fast recovery from fracture.
- Powdered *chanhawar* roots for fever and bodyache.
- Paste of leaves of *imli* (tamarind) to control vomiting and loose motions.

such as—cough and cold, malaria, tuberculosis, diarrhoea and skin disorders. Some of them are as follows:

1. Malaria is caused due to persistent cough and cold.
2. Stomach disorders lead to malaria.
3. Skin disorders are hereditary in nature.
4. Water deficiency in body causes tuberculosis.
5. Malaria is caused by evil spirits that only *Ojha* is able to get rid off.
6. Grains produced by chemical fertilisers cause tuberculosis.
7. Excessive consumption of *gur* and sweet causes tuberculosis.
8. A weak mother will make child susceptible to diarrhoea.
9. Use of brinjal (eggplant) causes skin disorders.

In order to explore the level of understanding of aetiology of common diseases, this study attempted to ask a few questions on perception of reasons behind different diseases. Table 7.10 shows the results. It exhibits that despite prevalence of several misconceptions among the respondents the understanding of the causes of malaria is good and this can be attributed to awareness programmes launched by both the government departments and the Ashram. The awareness of causes of the other diseases is rather poor. In this respect there is very little difference between the Ashram and the non-Ashram villages.

Table 7.10: Frequency of Correct Understanding about Causes of Diseases and their Prevention

Correct reason	Ashram Villages		Non-Ashram villages		Total	
	No.	%	No.	%	No.	%
N	603		201		804	
Cause of malaria	443	73.47	158	78.61	601	74.75
Ways of malaria prevention	308	51.08	107	53.23	415	51.62
Cause of diarrhoea	146	24.21	69	34.33	215	26.74
Ways of diarrhoea prevention	112	18.57	48	23.88	160	19.90
Cause of TB	102	16.92	30	14.93	132	16.42
Ways of TB prevention	14	2.32	1	0.50	15	1.87
Cause of skin problems	307	50.91	98	48.76	405	50.37
Ways of skin problem prevention	235	38.97	78	38.81	313	38.93

Source: Adult Schedule.

7.14 Family Planning

The Ashram has worked for decades in creating awareness amongst people about family planning. The message given to people was even broader than family planning and touched all aspects of happy family life. In this direction, the book written by Dr. Ragini Prem 'Parivar Sukh Kaise' was a significant step in which she explained in detail about the concept of safe period and tried to remove the misconceptions people had. In 1993 a mass reach programme was launched with the help of 82 Gram Sakhis and women who formed 42 groups. They went on foot to villages in groups and talked to women about problems of increasing population, family planning and other related issues.

The household data collected in the study shows that there are 4.71 births per woman in Ashram area. The number of births in the non-Ashram areas is also same. The survey shows that nearly 50 per cent of the adult population does not use any family planning method. Table 7.11 shows the use of different methods. Female sterilisation is by far the most common method used and even in the Ashram villages only one in twenty uses safe period method for family planning.

Table 7.11: Use of Family Planning Methods

Method	*Ashram Villages*		*Non Ashram Villages*		*Total*	
	No.	*%*	*No.*	*%*	*No.*	*%*
N	185		67		252	
Female sterlisation	90	48.65	48	71.64	138	54.76
Safe period method	11	5.95	5	7.46	16	6.35
Pills	7	3.78	0	0.00	7	2.78
Condoms	6	3.24	1	1.49	7	2.78
Others	29	15.68	2	2.99	31	12.30
Non-response	42	22.70	11	16.42	53	21.03

Source: Adult Schedule.

Awareness about some new risks such as HIV/AIDS is poor. Only 45.69 per cent respondents in Ashram area know about HIV/AIDS as compared to 66.00 per cent in the non-Ashram area. As maintained by many Gandhian workers the Ashram believes that HIV/AIDS occurs due to immoral behaviour. The Ashram seems to be unwilling about taking up awareness of HIV among young adults thinking that this may lead to inappropriate conduct. The Ashram does not want to talk about condoms etc. among adolescents and young adults.

7.15 Formation of VHSC

One of the major components of the National Rural Health Mission (NRHM) is to involve the local people in health delivery system. This is to be achieved through formation of Village Health and Sanitation Committees (VHSC) which have a number of functions. Table 7.11 shows that as reported by ASHAs, most villages have a VHSC, though not all of them seem to be functioning well. In this respect the Ashram villages seem to be lagging behind the non-Ashram villages. However, the table needs to be interpreted with care. ASHAs being part of the government's health programme are likely to exaggerate the functioning of government health institutions and downplay the achievements of the Ashram and other NGOs. The reality could be different and seems to be different.

The Ashram has adopted the policy of capacity building. As part of the Ashram's policy to build links with public administration, the Ashram has reached an agreement with HINDALCO hospital for difficult deliveries. Arrangements have been made that all patients will be taken care of. Thus Ashram acts in multiple ways: (a) it promotes positive traditional practices but attacks superstitions and magic; (b) it promotes natural delivery; and (c) in emergency helps the mothers through building agreements with government and non-government organizations.

Table 7.12: VHSC Formation

VHSC	*Ashram Villages*		*Non-Ashram Villages*		*Total*	
	No.	*%*	*No.*	*%*	*No.*	*%*
N	28		19		47	
VHSC is formed	22	78.57	18	94.74	40	85.11
VHSC is active	14	63.64	16	88.89	30	75.00

Source: ASHA Schedule.

7.16 Conclusion

The health interventions of the Ashram are more in the form of fighting superstitions and magic and developing a self-reliant model of health care. Thus the Ashram approach is marked by a certain degree of ambivalence towards the modern health care. It does not reject the modern health system (for example, treatment of malaria, started with government support, is still continued, and Arogya Kendra continues to provide services to poor patients even from the neighbouring states) but attempts to develop a way of healthy living in areas where the reach or effectiveness of the modern (allopathic) system is rather limited. At no stage the Ashram had enough financial, manpower, or other resources to develop an effective health intervention in the project area. The Ashram villages suffer from high morbidity from major diseases and malaria is still a killer disease, yet Ashram has shown the way by combining indigenous and modern systems of health leading to a *pragmatic and plural* approach to health care. There is a caveat here. Once the Ashram interventions are withdrawn (due to shortage of funds) the progress made by the Ashram may not be sustained and the people will become more dependent on the inadequate and unreliable medical system or on the traditional healers or *Jhola Chaap* doctors. The good work done by the Ashram needs to be sustained with support from government and non-government organizations. The type of agreement reached with HINDALCO is a welcome move in that direction.

CHAPTER 8

Social and Environmental Issues

When the Ashram started its activities there were several social problems that plagued the villages. The tribes were naïve and ignorant. They were subjugated and dominated by the "civilized people". The liquor mafia was promoting consumption of liquor. Moneylending was a roaring business. Tribals took loan from money lenders by mortgaging their land, and fell in the debt trap. Slavery and bonded labour were there in a large number of villages. The Ashram saw it as an urgent problem to address. The tribal people were cut-off from the larger political processes and ideas of progress and civilization. As with other tribes they practiced animism and lived in a state of helplessness.

The local population was divided into distinct castes and tribes. There were conflicts between them and the position of women was deplorable. Though historically in a tribal society status of women has been higher than in the non-tribal communities, due to effects of outside forces the situation changed. Women became victims of violence. Men drank heavily and in a state of intoxication picked up fights and indulged in wife beating. Women were also victims of witch hunting. The Ashram observed that due to their ignorance, illiteracy and subordination, they worked at much lower wages. In this context, empowering women appeared to be an urgent issue. Thus giving women education and skills, and eradiation of social evils came on top of the Ashram's agenda.

Seventies onwards Sonbhadra saw setting up of dams and power plants. This displaced hundreds of villages and deprived thousands of families from their habitat and livelihood. Rapid industrialisation disturbed the fragile ecology, leading to depletion of forest cover and rise in pollution. The Ashram came to the forefront and addressed the issues concerning environment and ecological degradation of the area. This chapter is devoted to above three issues: fighting social evils, women empowerment, and environmental action.

8.1 Eradication of Social Evils

The Ashram addressed the problem of liquor mafia operating in the villages and demanded closure of *bhatties* (furnaces) in the villages. It worked for the release of bonded labour and eradication of child labour in the carpet industry. The problem of *dayan pratha* (witch tradition) was addressed through creation of social awareness and improvement in status of women.

8.1.1 Liquor Consumption

Traditionally in the tribal areas both men and women consumed liquor. It was part of their everyday life. Even very young children were given liquor. Liquor was made locally in village *bhatties* and several people brewed it at home also. The licences of *bhatties* were mostly with Jaiswals who are known as liquor barons in the state. The Ashram saw that people indulged in petty quarrels and wife beating when intoxicated. The Ashram's major effort in the area was to eradicate consumption of liquor completely. In the seventies and eighties a movement was launched to create awareness among people to stop taking liquor. The environment was highly charged when the local people, particularly women, got involved in closure of liquor *bhatties* and liquor selling shops.

(a) Drive Against Liquor Consumption

The Ashram launched a series of drives against liquor consumption. This made villagers oppose setting up of new liquor shops in their village. Shubhaji tells that whereever villagers became conscious, they collectively threw the liquor shop out of their village. One can see that that licensed shops are out of the village, and in town area, and have not yet entered the village. In the year 2005, a liquor baron obtained licence for setting up country liquor shop at the Ashram *Mod*, in Myorepur block. The shop was set up in a rented premise, stocks were builtup and the shop got inaugurated. People were against this. According to Jagat Narayan, President of Vyapar Mandal "there are *bhatties* in the village that we won't care about. But we won't allow someone to come here on the road and set up a liquor shop. We don't want promotion of liquor." Soon people got together to oppose this and 35 shop keepers came forward to take up the cause. The shopkeepers' association wrote to Dr. Ragini Prem and sought her support. People got collected and *gheraoed* (covered) the shop. Women came in large number. They invited the media to cover the news. Pressure was applied on the landlord who had rented the shop to the liquor mafia. Looking at the intense opposition, next day the shop was closed down. According to a shopkeeper "The Ashram is like a guardian to us, always there when we need it." Shopkeepers have learnt that recently an advertisement has come out again for auction of liquor shop at the Ashram *Mod*. At the time of the study, plans were on anvil to take collective action against opening of liquor shop there again. Similar stories echoed from several villages. Peopie did not allow liquor shops to be set up in their villages.

(b) Preventing Production and Sale of Liquor Inside the Villages

The Ashram took keen interest in mobilizing people against production and sale of liquor inside the villages. Vimalji recalls: "In Nava Tola country liquor was produced and sold in Chhattisgarh state, across the border. The Ashram organised peaceful opposition to production of liquor throughout this region. Awareness camps were planned regularly with support from the local people. Soon people realised how much amount of wealth they are drinking away. Collectively people gheraoed the liquor *bhatti* and formed a circular human chain 100 mt away from *bhatti* with *bhatti* in the centre, and did not allow buyers to reach and come out of the *bhatti*. We were told never to attacks and hold only a peaceful demonstration. After the *bhatti* got removed, a school was inaugurated for children. Nearly 25 *bhatties* were closed down using peaceful demonstrations which lasted for several months. The campaign organised by Rajmohini Mata (an influential tribal prophetess who became a devoted disciple of Gandhi) also gave a big impetus to eradicating liquor. People declared a ban on the sale and consumption of liquor." The job was not easy but was achieved with support from local people who had started respecting the Ashram people by then for their help during the famine and for fighting for the tribals to secure their land and forest rights. Shiv Sharanji, a senior Ashram worker, recalls how dangerous it was to take a head-on battle against liquor mafia. The Ashram could win the battle only with support from the local people.

(c) Lack of Sustained Efforts

The fight to curb liquor production and consumption was on for a few decades. The fight had a social, a religious, a spiritual and a political substratum. Lakhs of followers of Raj Mohini Mata took vow to abstain from consumption of meat and liquor. And there was a general climate against liquor. However, in the mid-nineties, the liquor shops started getting auctioned in the district by government. The Ashram seemed to lose battle against government, liquor barons and forces of modernization. The general acceptability of liquor and tobacco grew again. In this context, to see the present status of consumption of liquor and other substance use, data were collected through the adult and young persons' schedules. Table 8.1 shows the findings of the analysis.

Table 8.1: Substance Use

Substance use	*Ashram villages*		*Non-Ashram villages*		*Total*	
	No.	*%*	*No.*	*%*	*No.*	*%*
Adult schedule						
N	603		201		804	
Smoke bidi or cigarette	61	10.12	24	11.94	85	10.57
Consume tobacco	281	46.60	105	52.24	386	48.01
Take liquor	216	35.82	51	25.37	267	33.21
Young people schedule						
N	151		50		201	
Smoke bidi or cigarette	25	4.15	3	1.49	28	3.48
Consume tobacco	8	1.33	2	1.00	10	1.24
Take liquor	46	7.63	14	6.97	60	7.46

The table exhibits that there is again a high incidence of tobacco consumption in the region. About every second person smokes or takes tobacco in some form or the other. The substance use in the Ashram villages matches, and in case of liquor exceeds that in the non-Ashram villages. It could be concerning that the liquor consumption among youth, though not so high at the moment, is rising. The reported trend of consumption by adults and Sarpanchs is in the same direction. Both, adult respondents and Sarpanchs said that the consumption of liquor is on rise everywhere—in the Ashram villages and the non-Ashram villages.

Table 8.2: Trends in Liquor Consumption

Trends	*Ashram villages*		*Non-Ashram villages*		*Total*	
	No.	*%*	*No.*	*%*	*No.*	*%*
Adult schedule						
N	603		201		804	
Consumption is increasing*	521	86.40	174	86.57	695	86.44
Consumption is stable	30	4.98	11	5.47	41	5.10
Consumption is decreasing	48	7.96	11	5.47	59	7.34
Consumption has stopped	1	0.17	3	1.49	4	0.50
Cannot say	3	0.50	2	1.00	5	0.62
Sarpanch schedule						
N	30		10		40	
Consumption is increasing*	23	76.67	10	100.00	33	82.50
Consumption is stable	4	13.33	0	0.00	4	10.00
Consumption is decreasing	3	10.00	0	0.00	3	7.50
Consumption has stopped	0	0.00	0	0.00	0	0.00
Cannot say	0	0.00	0	0.00	0	0.00

* The difference between the Ashram and the Non-ashram blocks is significant at 5 per cent level of significance.

The analysis of data collected through the adult schedule shows that the expenditure per family per month on various substances such as tobacco, liquor and *pan masala* is Rs 137.43 in the Ashram villages and Rs. 142.76 in non-Ashram villages. The difference is, however, very small to be noticed.

Thus it may be said that much of the Ashram's efforts in getting liquor banned in the project area and educating people about its ill effects, seem to be losing the effect. Use of tobacco and *pan masala* is also on rise. The Ashram has been attempting to address these issues among the adolescents through the Kishor-Kishori Sahjeevan Shivir. But in the general population there is a reverse trend. What was considered to be an evil earlier seems to have become acceptable. Some respondents attribute this to modernity, others to lack of meaningful work in the villages. Vested interests in sale of liquor are certainly a factor in this.

8.1.2 Moneylending

At the time Ashram started its activities, tribals were in the trap of moneylenders who took away their land or held them in bondage. Dr. Ragini Prem recalls how tribals were exploited by the moneylenders and how they were made to resist against them (moneylenders) but could never come out of the debt bondage for generations. There were two kinds of moneylenders in the area: Pathans and Rouniyars. Some Pathans, hailing from Lucknow, had a strong hold in this region. They visited the villages frequently and gave loans at exorbitant rates. They collected high interest and in case someone is unable to pay off they forcibly took away any assets from his house. Often farmers were made to agree to give away their standing crops to them to repay the debt. Pathans, who were called the *Lucknowa*, were detested by the local people but they had no option and they were afraid of their (moneylenders) power.

Rouniyars or Roniaur *bania* are Jaiswals who were originally from Bihar and Jharkhand. They are also known as Namnihar. In Bihar they are mostly engaged in trading of grains. After independence and land reforms, they migrated out in large numbers to settle in Sonbhadra, Varanasi and Mirzapur districts. The debt bondage was actually introduced by them. Many of them own land in the area and have shops also but their business thrived on moneylending. They rarely cultivated their own land and gave it to tenets under sharecropping. In the past tribals practiced subsistence economy. They largely depended on agriculture and forest for living. Tribals had very little to eat during the two-three monsoon months when they survived on Mahua and Chakwad. Namnihars were traders of foodgrains and they easily offered people food to gain sympathy. These were always the difficult months for tribals when

Namnihars kindly offered them advances. Tribals were too innocent to realise the trap set by the wily moneylenders. They sometimes gave their ready crops of arhar at throw away prices. When unable to pay back the debt, they lost their land and valuable assets to the moneylenders, and became bonded labours. Moneylenders used muscle and coercive means to create their influence and terror in the region that tribals could not dare to challenge.

Around 1970, the Ashram worked for the release of land of bonded labour. The Ashram worked with the tribals and persuaded moneylenders to recalculate the debt and value of labour already put in. Dr. Ragini Prem recalls: "Tribals were very innocent. They did not understand the games played by moneylenders and their clever manipulations. When the Ashram started to get them released, some of them were so scarred that they came running from their village and took shelter with us. They were frightened of getting beaten up. Moneylenders had clout and tribals were worried getting arrested by police. Slowly they gathered courage and could stand up against atrocities." The Ashram taught them to remain united and face the moneylenders collectively. They were also given bullocks and fertilizers to earn their livelihood so that they do not succumb to debt trap again. Anil Kumar Jaiswal is 46 year old Rouniyar who lives in Chauna village (Babhni block). He narrates how his father lost a huge sum of money in 1977.

> We were moneylenders and controlled credit in the villages. We exercised great power. Nearly Rs. 3.5 lakh was loaned out to local villagers by my father. That time the Ashram became very active and confronted us (moneylenders). Government too supported them. The villagers refused to return the money. Our family was successful in applying pressure on the villagers to return back the money quickly. They knew very well that in the future they would have to come to our family for any emergency credit needs. But Ashram came in the way. We lost it all. Later our *bhatti* (liquor distillation) plant was also shut down under pressure from the Ashram.

At present there is no evidence of bonded labour in the district. The primary data show that about 44.11 per cent families in the

Ashram villages and 47.76 per cent families in the non-Ashram villages have taken loans. However, there is a significant difference in the amount of loan that each family has in Ashram and non-Ashram villages. The Ashram area respondents appear to be more careful in taking loan than those outside the Ashram activities.

Table 8.3: Extent and Amount of Loaning

Loan	*Ashram villages*		*Non-Ashram villages*		*Total*	
	No.	*%*	*No.*	*%*	*No.*	*%*
N	603		201		804	
Taken loan	266	44.11	96	47.76	362	45.02
Loan amount (₹)*	14,853.91		22,965.63		17,332.72	

* The difference between the Ashram and the Non-ashram blocks is significant at 5 per cent level of significance.

In rural area people take loans mostly for marriages and, treatment of illnesses, buying animals and requirements of agriculture. The source of loan is largely moneylenders, friends and relatives. The percentage of people who take loans from moneylenders in the Ashram and non-Ashram villages are 19.90 per cent and 17.41 per cent respectively. Considering that in the seventies almost everyone was in the clutches of moneylenders, situation seems to have much improved now. Surely there are no cases of bonded labour that we witness in the district.

> In Chouna village (block Babhni) there is a large Jaiswal community that is traditionally engaged in moneylending. Sixty per cent of the population of this village is that of tribals, dominated by Agaria, Kharwar, Gaur and Kol. In 1970s the tribals of the village were quite poor and had huge amount of loans from the moneylenders of their own village. Many of them (tribals) became bonded labour to repay the loan. Around 1977 Ashram started a movement for freeing bonded labour from moneylenders, which also covered this village.
>
> Today the situation has changed. The research team found that in this village only 15 per cent of the tribals took loans

from moneylenders. Also the amount was less than ₹ 5,000 in each case. This is a sum that they could easily pay off. The Jaiswals have good business, agriculture and dairies and they do not need to survive on moneylending business. One of them recalls how much of his loan money was lost due to interference of the Ashram. Sukhdeo, a Kharwar by caste remembers, "The Ashram freed us from moneylenders. We do not go to moneylenders any more. When I needed loan last year, I went to the local bank."

Photo 8.1: A poor farmer from the tribal area

8.1.3 Dayan Pratha (Witch Hunting)

As discussed in Chapter 7 the Ashram too has special interest in health. On the one hand it encouraged the use of endogenous knowledge systems and on the other fought against superstitions and magic. The Ashram took special interest in fighting the witch hunting which led to violence against women branded as witch for various reasons.

> Ramani got branded as a *dayan* (witch) by a local *Ojha*. Villagers called a panchayat and discussed the matter. Her husband was asked to get rid of her. When he refused to do so, both of them were banished from the village.

In the past many women faced physical and mental torture for no fault of their's. When because of their family problems or distress they behave violently and erratically, they get termed as a witch. After that they are ill treated by all people. They are physically tortured, beaten up and humiliated on the pretext that the *Ojha* has to get the witch off her body. Several cases like this are still heard in the villages of Sonbhadra—a woman was thrown into fire, her tongue was chopped off, hair was pulled and she was beaten up badly.

According to Shubhaji "*Never a man is declared a witch. It is always a woman who comes under the spell of an evil spirit. We know that it is mostly inspired by personal rivalry, jealousy or property reasons. There is no basis for it*". The Ashram took a strong stand on the matter of witchcraft, and told people to abandon such superstitious beliefs. The unfortunate part of this problem is that most of the time the victim is unable to seek help from villagers. Police and Sarpanch try to suppress such matters. Table 8.4 shows the perception of people about the trend in *dayan pratha*. Clearly everyone feels the trend is declining but individuals are more candid than the Sarpanchs about admitting that *dayan pratha* still exists in their village. The figures show that the Ashram villages have greater incidence of witch hunting than the non-Ashram villages despite a very positive role of the Ashram in eradicating this practice. There may be several reasons behind this: a stronger history of witch hunting, poverty, isolation, preponderance of tribal population, and lack of connectivity with the civilization. The researchers feel that the incidence of witch hunting is much higher than understood as many cases are simply not reported.

Table 8.4: Trend in *Dayan Pratha*

Item	*Ashram villages*		*Non-Ashram villages*		*Total*	
	No.	*%*	*No.*	*%*	*No.*	*%*
Adult schedule						
N	603		201		804	
Increasing	64	10.61	5	2.49	69	8.58
Stable and same as before	201	33.33	62	30.85	263	32.71
Decreasing	286	47.43	108	53.73	394	49.00
Eradicated	25	4.15	22	10.95	47	5.85
Cannot say	26	4.31	4	1.99	30	3.73
Sarpanch schedule						
N	30		10		40	
Increasing	3	10.00	0	0.00	3	7.50
Stable and same as before	7	23.33	0	0.00	7	17.50
Decreasing	20	66.67	9	90.00	29	72.50
Eradicated	0	0.00	1	10.00	1	2.50
Cannot say	0	0.00	0	0.00	0	0.00

Ram Roop and his wife had a dispute with their neighbour about the forest land he was cultivating in his village. When the fight became intense 28 people got together. They took the couple to an *Ojha* in Bindhamganj, on Jharkhand border. According to the couple this *Ojha* was bribed by the other farmer. Ram Roop was told that his wife was a witch. Villagers collected and decided to ostracize them. Anyone who visited them would be penalised ₹ 5000. Ram Roop filed a complaint with the police. After a few days police came to their village, and Ram Roop and his family could manage to stay in the village. Although the couple stays in the village, they are practically outside the village. No one ever visits them. The village children tease their kids and call them '*dayan bache*'.

8.2 Women Empowerment

Ashram used education and awareness to awaken and empower women. The Total Literacy Campaign (TLC) was a successful educational mission of the Ashram. The Akshar Sainiks were products of the Ashram schools, who were deputed to go to their village and educate at least five women each. Dr. Ragini Prem said: "The results were encouraging. Our own survey showed that the female literacy soared to 80 per cent." Girls started going to schools.

Gram Sakhis appointed by the Ashram, were linked with the village women. At the Vikas Manch level there were Sahyoginis. Women started getting networked through them, linking with the Ashram and its multifarious activities. They were taught composting, *agarbatti* making, pickle making and tailoring, etc. For the first time tribal women came out of their homes and experienced rise in aspirations to acquire more education and, move ahead.

Groups of women were formed. The people at the Ashram realised that the self-help groups (SHGs) formed under various government schemes were only to avail the monetary benefits of the programmes (such as revolving fund). Instead the Ashram laid emphasis on regular savings and inter-loaning. Shubhaji said: "We do not conduct monthly monetoring of the SHGs. The formation of SHGs was not our programme. We did not want to take up the whole responsibility of SHG. We worked as facilitator and motivator. In fact we talk about SHGs in our awareness campaign. We do not set targets for our volunteers. Only when women come forward and are ready for it, we help them form SHG." At present there are nearly 103 SHGs formed by the Ashram. Villages where the concept of SHGs has clicked, women have enjoyed more collective power.

Photo 8.2: Phoolwanti and her friends in Bagharu village (Babhni block) handle village problems collectively

Association of Phoolwanti of Bagharu (Babhni block) with the Ashram is very old. She has been associated with the Ashram since she got married and came to this village. She got training from the Ashram and works as a volunteer. About six years back she set up a successful SHG of 15 women, named Kasturba Samooh. Due to regular savings, inter-loaning and strict discipline the SHG functions well. None of the members now go to moneylender for credit. Together they raise voice against oppression and injustice and demand equal rights. Dhanman, a member of the group tells: "MNREGA work was given to contractor in our village, who got JCB machine to do the job. It was taking away our wage work and we opposed." One day 150 women of the village gathered and did not let machine move. Police was called by the village Sarpanch. Now the contractor had no choice but to back off. With pride women show their fields where farming is organic. They are determined not to use chemicals in their fields. Their village is located on the foothills, at the banks of Kanwar river. Illegal mining of sand from the river was going on. The forest contractor used to resort to illegal felling of trees. Members of the women SHG got organized and stopped the contractors from mining. They also approached forest officers and told them to stop illegal felling of trees on the hills. They protect their forests well and ensure that no one stops regeneration of forests in their village.

This study shows that the women of the Ashram villages are much more active now. Nearly one third women respondents are members of Gram Sabha, almost the same as in the non-Ashram villages. Table 8.5 shows that in the Ashram villages a higher percentage of women attend the Gram Sabha meetings.

Women were asked about who should take decisions in a family—husband, wife, both of them jointly or someone else. Analysis of data reveals that the women are mostly for democratic decision making, i.e. decisions taken jointly by husband and wife (Table 8.6). There were no significant differences between the Ashram and the non-Ashram areas.

The Ashram's work certainly gave confidence to women and it instilled a sense of achievement in them. They felt more empowered to raise their voices against injustice and oppression. Women started coming out in large numbers to attend meetings and discuss issues

Table 8.5: Membership of Gram Sabha and Attendance of Meetings by Women

Item	*Ashram villages*		*Non-Ashram villages*		*Total*	
	No.	*%*	*No.*	*%*	*No.*	*%*
Membership of Gram Sabha						
N	190		50		240	
Women	96	31.79	21	21.43	117	29.25
Men	94	31.23	29	28.16	123	30.45
Women who attend meeting of Gram Sabha						
Regularly	6	1.99	0	0.00	6	1.5
Sometimes	50	16.56	10	10.20	60	15
Never*	246	81.46	88	89.80	334	83.5

* Significant difference between the Ashram and the Non-Ashram villages at 5 per cent level of significance.

Source: Adult Schedule.

that relate to development and governance. Researchers observed a Gram Sawarajya meeting held at the Ashram where there was a good presence of women who walked all the way from their village to participate in the debate on environment. An interesting fact is that in any such gathering, unlike the city counterparts, men and women do not segregate, and they sit together. This is an achievement of Ashram.

8.3 Industrialisation and Pollution

The skyline of Sonbhadra has turned blackish grey in the last few decades due to pollution by factories. Village Bairpur (Chopan block) is 30 km away from Obra power plant. It receives fly ash from Obra and Anapara power plants. The greyish white deposits are clearly visible on the leaves of the trees. Health of goats feeding on these leaves has become bad. According to people, pollution has led to increased incidence of abortions among goats. Fruits of trees specially *mahua* and *chironjee* dropped down early. A greater proportion of new born children have physical and mental disabilities than in the past. The environment problem has taken a serious proportion and yet there is no action by government on this matter.

Table 8.6: Who Should Take Decision in the Family

(Per cent of women respondents)

Decisions and decision makers	*Ashram block*		*Non-ashram block*		*Total*	
	No.	*%*	*No.*	*%*	*No.*	*%*
N	603		201		804	
About domestic expense						
Husband	33	5.47	12	5.97	45	5.60
Wife	37	6.14	7	3.48	44	5.47
Both	525	87.06	181	90.05	706	87.81
Other	5	0.83	1	0.50	6	0.75
Missing	3	0.50	0	0	3	0.37
About woman going to her parents place						
Husband	61	10.12	23	11.44	84	10.45
Wife	16	2.65	6	2.99	22	2.74
Both	519	86.07	166	82.59	685	85.20
Other	4	0.66	6	2.99	10	1.24
Missing	3	0.50	0	0	3	0.37
About family planning						
Husband	9	1.49	1	0.50	10	1.24
Wife	17	2.82	10	4.98	27	3.36
Both	571	94.69	190	94.53	761	94.65
Other	3	0.50	0	0	3	0.37
Missing	3	0.50	0	0	3	0.37
About land purchase						
Husband	77	12.77	29	14.43	106	13.18
Wife	5	0.83	4	1.99	9	1.12
Both	510	84.58	158	78.61	668	83.08
Other	8	1.33	10	4.98	18	2.24
Missing	3	0.50	0	0	3	0.37
About education of children						
Husband	43	7.13	7	3.48	50	6.22
Wife	24	3.98	10	4.98	34	4.23
Both	529	87.73	183	91.04	712	88.56
Other	4	0.66	0	0	4	0.50
Missing	3	0.50	1	0.50	4	0.50

Source: Adult Schedule.

The Ashram has taken several initiatives to bring the problem of environmental pollution to the forefront. Rallies in the villages to *gosthis* (meetings) and seminars have helped generate awareness among people. During the survey when the adults were asked to compare the quality of air and water since the time they were young, 67.99 per cent of the people in Ashram villages said it has deteriorated (Fig. 8.1). As compared to this only 48.26 per cent adults in the

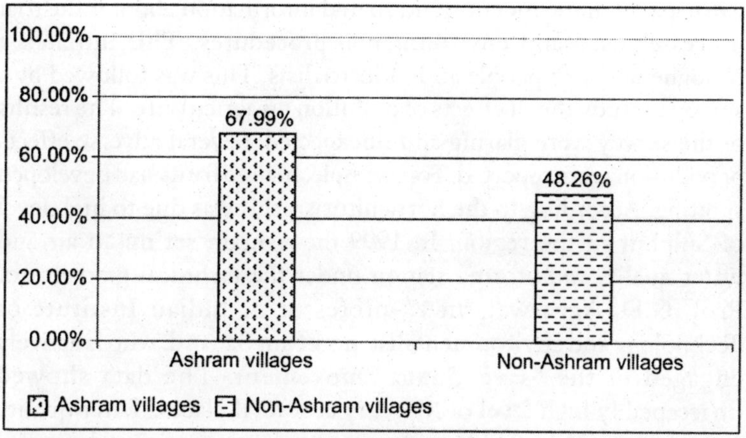

Fig. 8.1: Percentage of respondents who say the air and water quality in their village is not good

non-Ashram villages reported a drop in the quality. This could be either because of more pollution in the Ashram area or due to the higher concentration of factories there or because people in the Ashram area are more aware and have higher level of understanding about these issues.

Elderly people recall that since early sixties when Rihand dam came up, it caused a spurt in industrial activity in the area. By the end of sixties, Hindalco, Kanoria Chemical, Obra Dam, Renusagar Power Plant, Dala Cement Factory, Churk Cement Factory were on the landscape of Sonbhadra. Hundreds of crushers emerged in Renukoot and coal mining began at several places. These industrial activities caused exploitation of natural resources and massive displacement of people. Forests were cut to make place for industrial development. The skyline turned grey with the coal dust and ambient temperature rose up. Singrauli area got the term 'Energy Capital of India' but its people got high level of pollution, unemployment and displacement. Construction of Rihand Dam alone caused evacuation of 400 inhabited villages. For many of them their land compensation is still in process with the government.

In 1996 the Ashram called a meeting of representatives of industries and the local people to discuss the issues of pollution and displacement. A number of representatives of major industries participated in the meeting and shared information about industrial processes used and environmental procedures. This initiated a dialogue between people and industrialists. This was followed by a survey to study the ill effects of pollution on agriculture. The results of the survey were glaring and unexpected. Several adverse effects of pollution were reported. For example, mango fruits had developed spotting. According to the horticulturists this was due to high level of Sulphur in the region. In 1999 the Ashram set up an air and water quality monitoring station under the technical guidance of Prof. G.D. Aggarwal, an ex-professor of Indian Institute of Technology and environmentalist, now Sant Sanand, who is actively engaged in the "save Ganga" movement. The data showed unacceptably high level of Mercury at several places. Water quality testing showed high Fluoride content in water, in and around Beejpur. In the Myorepur area the industrial ash has raised prevalence of asthma among the local people. Clearly due to over exploitation of land and other natural resources, environment has been adversely affected. National Thermal Power Corporation (NTPC) provided filter machine to be fitted in with hand pumps, but they are so few in number that they do not cater to the needs of even one whole village. These efforts by major industries are like paying only a lip service to the environmental issues.

The Ashram attempted to draw attention of policy makers but the results are not much visible. The environment is badly affected by power plants, large manufacturing plants, and cement industry. The fruits from the trees grown locally have black spots and their yield has significantly declined. According to one older respondent "we used to have *chironjee* (a dry fruit grown in abundance in the past) for our meals. Our children do not have it even for *pooja* (worship)". People are experiencing rise in tuberculosis and asthma, but they are helpless and hapless. They have no answers, no direction.

8.4 Conclusion

This chapter presents the summary of the Ashram's efforts made in three fields: fighting social evils like substance use, women empowerment and dealing with environmental pollution. The study shows the mixed results. The Ashram has effectively fought against social evils such as liquor consumption and witch hunting, promoted women empowerment, and raised awareness about pollution. The Ashram is also involved in environmental monitoring. These efforts have produced some results. The practice of witch hunting has declined, though it has not been completely banished from the villages. Women have become more aware and more organized. They are more active politically and they participate in the village panchayats, more than in the area outside the influence of the Ashram. Gender discrimination and gender violence have reduced significantly. However, the Ashram's efforts in stopping production and sale of liquor which had a great success in the beginning seem to have failed, and in the recent years, use of liquor, tobacco, *pan masala* etc. has gone up. The Ashram's potential to give fight to liquor barons, government and other vested interests is limited. On the front of environment, people have become more aware but this is a problem which has to be tackled at the level of industrialists and not at the level of people. The Ashram is lacking in human and financial support to make an impact. The old support by the intellectuals, professionals, political leaders and activists is on decline. The administration has respect for the Ashram but lacks commitment and transparency, and due to corruption and expediency is unwilling to seek guidance from the Ashram. The industrialists would heed to law and government only and treat pollution as an unavoidable risk of development. The adverse consequences of industrialization are to be borne by lakhs of villagers but a small group of people who are beneficiaries of industrialization are more powerful than the ordinary villagers. It would be a very large task to organize people against the horrendous consequences of "development and modernization". In meetings and conferences Dr. Ragini Prem very convincingly agrees with Gandhi and argues that industrialization is perilous. Yet, everyone seems to be helpless and clueless.

CHAPTER 9

Achievements, Limitations and Future Directions

There is no doubt that the development activities of the Ashram have made a positive contribution to the welfare and development of the region, particularly of the southern part of district Sonebhadra. The preceding chapters show the details of various interventions made by the Ashram in diverse fields. It has come out well that the multifaceted contact with villagers has been of primary importance to the sustainable development of the people. This chapter attempts to answer the questions raised in the beginning of the study. Thus this chapter attempts to identify major achievements and limitations of the Agrindus project, followed by suggestions regarding the future role of the Ashram

A. Does ideology mediate the impact of interventions on well-being of people? Specifically, do the ideas of *Swaraj* and *Sarvodaya* lead to a sense of well-being among people?

Yes, the importance of ideology cannot be underestimated. The most important achievements of the Ashram have been rooted in their ideological foundation of Gandhian thought. Through the ideology of *Sarvodaya* and *Swaraj* the Ashram has been able to do a number of things: (a) successfully fighting against casteism, untouchability and gender discrimination and promoting equality; (b) promoting participatory model of development; (c) eradicating social evils like *dayan* tradition and magic and witchcraft while retaining useful health traditions; (d) promoting non-violent and yet effective *Satyagraha* for rights and entitlements; and (e) making people sensitive to requirements of sustainable development. The backbone of the Ashram approach being the idea of *Sarvodaya* and *Swaraj* the Ashram has been able to achieve much more than what any other organization could do within the limitations of resources. It was also because of noble thought of rural reconstruction along the Gandhian lines that the Ashram was able to draw attention of a few leading jurists, academicians, activists, planners, scientists, doctors and media persons from both India and abroad and link the experts with masses. Ideology helped the Ashram in several ways:

- Presenting a clear vision and mission to the Ashram.
- A clear analysis of the problems of tribal and rural society.
- Building a trusting relationship with people.
- Involving people in decisions about themselves, i.e. promoting the participatory nature of development.
- Maintaining a high degree of intrinsic motivation among the Ashram workers for rural development without expecting any material reward in return. The Ashram has had the benefit of having full time workers who were well educated and trained.
- Getting human and financial resources from Gandhian and other donors interested in integrated rural development without bothering about immediate targets and sectoral allocations. The donors too had a high level of trust in the Ashram that they would use the donations efficiently for overall development of the tribal and rural communities.
- Looking for holistic and long term solutions.
- Developing a non-confrontalist, non-dualist model of development by involving all sections of society. In every sector the Ashram tried to eradicate the evil practices and approaches without rejecting the traditions completely. For example, the Ashram did not insist on institutional delivery though it made women aware of wrong traditions and requirements of safe motherhood (appropriate application of *haldi*, *gur* etc. and use of a new blade to cut the umbilical

cord). The Ashram fought against superstitions while promoting herbal and home remedies.

- Maintaining transparency and a high degree of integrity among functionaries, workers and volunteers. No doubt there have been a few isolated cases of forgery and fraud on the Ashrams but an overwhelming majority of functionaries and workers have worked with integrity, conviction and great enthusiasm for a long time. This has earned a great respect of the people/clients and the people of the project area evince a great confidence in the Ashram.

B. In the light of recent development efforts made by the state, does the Ashram need to reformulate its strategies or change some of its priorities? Where should they focus more?

Yes. The Ashram needs to reformulate its strategies. Over the years the impact of the Ashram is on decline. For example, between 1968 and 1996 the Ashram ran a number of programmes in the field of education. They included opening of a large number of primary schools, *prodh siksha* (adult literacy covering home schools for females and evening schools for males), opening libraries, Balmandir for age group 3-6 years, *Graminshala* for 7-14 years, and *Jeevanshala* (life school). They had a good participation of people. Literacy level reached nearly 80 per cent. However, for the present generation it has become a history. The gains could not be sustained. After 1996 the Ashram schools started closing down. As of today, school enrolment has declined and drop out rate has increased. Also there is more drop out among girls than boys. In certain Ashram villages such as Bairpur (block Chopan) where the Ashram has run its awareness programme school drop out rate among girls has increased to 77.2 per cent. Same is now story of even those villages where the Ashram had focused activities, night schools and life schools. In focused villages of the Ashram 18-20 per cent girls aged 18-20 are found to be outside the school. Overall, 39 per cent girls and 32 per cent boys are outside the school.

In general, the Ashram villages have been facing the condition of drought for more than five years. There is no doubt that industrialization created new opportunities for the rural youths outside agriculture and MNREGA provided 100 days of employment for the rural families on demand. Various government and the Ashram schemes have contributed to land development, agricultural development and improvement of irrigation facilities. However, due to inadequate employment situation, rising aspirations, craze for new gadgets like mobile phone, desire to wear Western dress (jeans), and competition youth are migrating to urban areas outside the state—more towards Punjab, Haryana and Delhi. Parental authority is weakening and there is no control of the old on the youth. Yet, a majority of respondents in both the Ashram and non-Ashram villages state that if they can get a job in the village itself they would not like to outmigrate. Moreover, it is notable that the migrant youths return to their village during agricultural seasons when there is a demand for their labour in the village.

The Ashram can do two things: promote the philosophy of *Swaraj* and *Sarvodaya*; and take up development projects to show how the development projects can be launched with a different framework and what do they achieve?

The Ashram also needs to link up with public administration, industry, and business houses to enable them to get feedback on their activities and develop socially and environmentally more responsible approaches. *However, this requires recruitment of professionally trained staff with support from and networking with various national and international agencies. The old volunteers with traditional training and thinking will not be able to do this kind of work.* There has been a good beginning in the recent past. The Ashram has sent its workers and the *Sarovodaya* volunteers, working in different parts of the country under Mahatma Gandhi Mission to get professional training in project writing, data analysis and project planning to places like IIT, Kanpur. One such workshop was organized in year 2004 on Project Methodology for the workers of the Ashram and other voluntary organizations. Another Two-day Workshop on Methodology of Writing Reports was held in the same year for secretaries of grassroots organizations working under Mahatma Gandhi Mission Scheme. Such efforts need to be enhanced. This will also connect the Ashram to professionals and possibly some of them may by change of heart be part of the Ashram activities in the future.

C. How can the state and NGOs work synergistically in the interest of people's development?

State is not a unified, simple system. It consists of layers of bureaucracy, police, political system and legal justice. To work in the interest of people is to work selflessly and single mindedly towards development. Yet with poor governance, inefficient administration and with political leaders themselves to be working in the interest of party or themselves the sate only launches the development projects on paper. Newspapers and other media reports are full of cases of corruption and leakages in the projects. Many NGOs which are dependent on government funds are also unclean and ineffective. Yet, organizations like the Banwasi Seva Ashram can show the way. The Ashram will be happy to work for environmental programme in a participatory manner with the State Government.

State can take the help of NGOs like the Banwasi Seva Ashram for a number of things: (a) as a consultant for prioritizing the needs of interventions; (b) as a group of workers for reaching the clients, and building rapport; (c) for developing local solutions; (d) for better governance; and (e) for reformulating development strategies. There is no doubt that in areas where the Ashram has done the ideological and mobilization work the rural development schemes can be run more efficiently.

With the construction of the Rihand dam the area started industrializing. The forests were felled blindly. Around the dam, in Myorepur block six thermal power plants were established. Then a cement factory was opened in Dala. This was followed by opening of a number of crushers. A number of large manufacturing units such as Aluminium factory, High Tech Carbon, Kanodia Chemicals and their ancilliaries were also opened. Thus an area known for forest reserves, and full of lakes and fountains, was turned into an urban space. The power elite took up the land belonging to simple tribal people—giving them allurement of secured jobs. The people did not get jobs but lost their land. They became labourers. Industrialization destroyed the environment. Pollution level increased and started impacting nature, agriculture, people, animals, flora and fauna. Due to excessive use of coal, amount of mercury has gone up in the atmosphere. This is polluting air, water and environment. The levels of chlorine, sulphur dioxide and nitrogen have also increased. In 1996 the Ashram took the initiative to control pollution.

The Ashram organized seminars on production technologies and raised awareness of adverse effects of pollution. This was followed by a survey of impact of pollution on agricultural productivity. The Ashram took help of two Ph.D. students to measure quality of water and air. They ware guided by renowned professor of environment, Prof. G.D. Agarwal. The findings of the experiments were shared with the people, administration and industry. Since 2002 the Ashram is working in close cooperation of the Central Pollution Board. It was found that at several places mercury, chlorine, sulphur dioxide and nitrogen were going beyond the permissible limits. Village dams and Pant Sagar Jalasaya had a large quantity of mercury and fluoride. Subsequently in year 2006 it was found that the pollution has severely impacted the farm and forest produce, production of fruits. Guavas, mangoes, *sharifas*, *kathals*, and pulses like *arhar* and *urd* were worse affected. Attempts were made to seek cooperation of industry and government in identifying fluoride and removing it. The area is facing enormous pollution problem due to different reasons and affecting health of the people. The efforts made by the government health department are notional and ineffective. On a few occasions NTPC has distributed filter machines and sometimes health department has written on some handpumps that the water is not drinkable. The Ashram has undertaken awareness drive. People are aware of the problem but have no solution. The state can take the advantage of the Ashram works to build a sound environmental programme in a participatory manner.

D. What have been the priorities in development in villages under Asharm activities and other villages?

It appears that while initially the Ashram focused more on survival and provision of food, gradually the activities of the Ashram were aimed at self-reliance. Therefore, the Ashram took up diverse activities including institution building, agricultural development, training and employment, strengthening of rural industry, education, health, protection of land rights, social integration, awareness, empowerment and environment. The study shows that in the project area the Ashram is known more for its contribution towards protection of land rights, and awareness programmes. People respect the Ashram functionaries for their selfless services and for showing the light to the one time isolated and ignorant masses.

The Ashram has fought relentlessly against social evils like witchcraft and sorcery. In 1970s the condition of women was deplorable. With a *dayan* tradition in existence people killed women on the pretext of their acting as *dayan* (witch). The village society was characterized by physical violence against women, abduction of women in the name of marriage, polygamy, wage difference, sexual discrimination, lack of interest in women's health, and lack of participation of women in social and cultural matters. The Ashram did many things for the upliftment of women. One of the major interventions in this direction was to improve women's education. In the local schools with local teachers it was decided that each youth taught in the school would teach five girls. As a result of this the level of literacy among girls rose to more than 60 per cent in a short period of time. Appointment of Gram Sakhis at the village level, Sahyoginis at the block level, and mobilization of women was another major intervention. In the meetings women were told about sustainable agricultural practices, natural farming, preparing green manure, importance of women's independence, minimum wages, women's rights, need for savings, economic activities they can take up (such as making of pickles, incense sticks, and soaps, and stitching of clothes). Even at the time of the survey under the scheme Mahila Chetna Vikas Gram Sakhis were telling women about making of compost khad. In Faripan village of block Myorepur women have dugged many pits and they are making compost khad. In this village 80 per cent villagers are involved in sustainable agriculture. Gram Sakhis are also involved in spreading health awareness, particularly causes and treatment of seasonal diseases, and safe motherhood. This led to increased self-confidence among women and assertion of their rights, whether in NREGA or in other schemes. They took decisive action in cases of inappropriate use of machines by contractors under rural development schemes, non-payment of wages in time, and illegal felling of plants by forest contractors in connivance with the officers. Kishor-Kishori Sahjivan Camps (for boys and girls aged 16-20 years) were organized in the Ashram for providing moral education, life skills, knowledge of biological changes among boys and girls, and eradicating substance use—*gutka*, *bidi*, cigarette, and liquor.

E. What is the difference in objective and subjective measures of well-being between Ashram villages and other villages?

Satisfaction and happiness are subjects of serious academic discussion. Well-being has both an objective component based on material condition and a subjective component of wellness. It is common to divide the determinants of happiness and satisfaction into two groups: satisfaction with respect to the economic condition, and a happy emotional state (which may include spiritual peace also).

The cash needs of people can be used as a proxy to economic self-reliance of villages. In this model of self-reliance the social groups consume each other's produce and exchange labour. The money people have stays back in the village. As Dr. Ragini Prem states: "even now there is a tradition in our villages to help each other out in doing *chappar-chavani* (repair of roofs). People take turns and work for each other. For this no one has to pay for the labour charges."

During the primary survey, respondents were asked about the expenses made by them monthly on various items. Their answers are analysed and presented in the tables below. Table 9.1 shows the responses of adults, Table 9.2 of the younger respondents.

This survey shows that in expenditure there was no noticeable difference between the Ashram and the non-Ashram villages. The average household expenditure in both the Ashram villages and the non-Ashram villages is ₹ 2,100 per month, ₹ 2,130 in the Ashram blocks, and ₹ 2,110 in the non-Ashram blocks (Table 9.1). However, there is a significant difference in the composition of the consumption. Compared to the villages outside the project area of the Ashram, the households in the Ashram villages spend more money on food, courts and housing and less on conveyance, medical/

health, education, petrol/diesel, mobile phones, electricity, clothing, animals, liquor or other substance uses, cosmetics, marriages and agriculture. The Ashram villages have lesser menace of gambling and substance use. They have also largely stopped the dowry payments. They spend more on housing because they lack the *pucca* houses as outside the project area and they want to build more

Table 9.1: Average Expense Incurred Monthly

(*In* ₹)

Item	*Ashram block*	*Non-ashram block*
Food	247.36 (305.29)	232.64 (226.05)
Conveyance	181.75 (183.94)	215.54 (200.25)
Medical	166.56 (223.93)	198.81 (161.45)
Education	214.38 (430.37)	220.37 (179.68)
Petrol/diesel	102.28 (168.89)	130.90 (187.12)
Mobile	141.97 (155.18)	204.84 (218.21)
Electricity	145 (75)	150 (70.71)
Clothing	230.46 (207.04)	244.36 (176.02)
Animal	86.96 (74.82)	145 (200.31)
Liquor/tobacco/*pan masala*	136.43 (186.04)	160.55 (373.98)
Other	285.55 (300.10)	332.72 (286.65)
Cosmetic	81.71 (53.76)	100.47 (82.88)
Marriage	177.68 (206.65)	234 (167.03)
Court cases	675 (350)	300 (251.82)
Agriculture inputs	239.16 (285.79)	300 (332.57)
House rent and maintenance	358.11 (469.02)	121.42 (76.67)
Average expense (per month)	2129.97 (1294.67)	2110.15 (1277.37)

Note: Figures in the brackets are standard deviation.
Source: Adult Schedule.

spacious, traditional houses made of local material. Babu Ram, a school teacher at Faripan (Babhni) says: "Now people are spending much more than before. Mobile phone, TV, watch and other goods have become needs of the youths today. Agriculture cannot give them enough cash and so they end up migrating out."

Young persons report a noticeably lower figures for the monthly expenditure (Table 9.2). In case of young persons a significantly lower expenditure is reported by the Ashram blocks as compared to the non-Ashram blocks.

Table 9.2: Average Expense Incurred Annually

(In ₹)

Item	*Ashram block*	*Non-ashram block*
Food	443.72 (543.86)	314.29 (69.01)
Conveyance	115.00 (94.55)	196.88 (255.80)
Medical	80.00 (96.03)	0.00 (0.00)
Education	225.58 (205.78)	242.86 (123.92)
Petrol/diesel	590.00 (562.35)	0.00 (0.00)
Mobile	223.88 (246.28)	210.71 (117.13)
Clothing	105.34 (125.03)	115.36 (97.34)
Liquor/tobacco/*pan masala*	195.10 (237.67)	187.50 (94.65)
Other	100.51 (103.67)	112.00 (81.62)
Cosmetic	62.94 (60.94)	76.88 (74.87)
House maintenance	442.86 (78.68)	400.00 (0.00)
Average expenditure (per month)	471.83 (688.03)	581.10 (617.03)

Note: Figures in the brackets are standard deviation
Source: Young Schedule.

Sometimes the figures hide the reality. For example, the figures that the residents of Ashram villages are as much involved in legal disputes and court cases as the residents of the villages outside the Ashram activities are misleading. According to qualitative interviews, the reason is that in a large number of cases in the Ashram area disputes relate to a few unresolved legal issues over land rights. They have arisen in the process of implementation of land rights and these cases have been pending for years. In these areas cases of criminal disputes, atrocities, dowry, faction fights and personal disputes are much less compared to non-Ashram villages. In the

Ashram areas such disputes get resolved at the village level itself through intervention of the village people and Ashram workers.

Yet, the observations show that the residents of the Ashram villages are more contended and happier despite facing drought for 3-4 years. Outside the Ashram despite better irrigation facilities and more prosperous agriculture people look less contended. They want more. Tables 9.3 and 9.4 show the degree of satisfaction with house and satisfaction in general.

Table 9.3: Satisfaction with House

Variable	*Ashram blocks*		*Non-Ashram blocks*		*Total*	
	No.	*%*	*No.*	*%*	*No.*	*%*
N	603		201		804	
Satisfied with house	327	54.23	76	37.81	403	50.12
N	151		50		201	
Satisfied with house	91	60.26	22	44.00	113	56.22

Note: Based on schedule of adult people. (first block)

Note: Based on schedule of young people. (second block)

Table 9.4: Satisfaction with Economic Condition

Variable	*Ashram blocks*		*Non-Ashram blocks*		*Total*	
	No.	*%*	*No.*	*%*	*No.*	*%*
N	603		201		804	
Yes	287	47.60	81	40.30	368	45.77
No	306	50.75	118	58.71	424	52.74
Don't say	10	1.66	2	1.00	12	1.49

Note: Based on schedule of adult people.

Analysis of survey data reveals:

- 47.60 per cent respondents in the Ashram villages are satisfied with their economic condition. The corresponding figure for the non-Ashram villages is 40.30. The difference is statistically insignificant.
- 54.23 per cent adult respondents in the Ashram villages are satisfied with the house. The corresponding figure for the

non-Ashram villages is 37.81. The difference is statistically significant at 5 per cent level of significance.

- 60.26 per cent young respondents in the Ashram villages are satisfied with the house. The corresponding figure for the non-Ashram villages is 44.00. The difference is statistically significant at 5 per cent level of significance.
- 45.69 per cent young respondents in the Ashram villages report that they see their future to be good (or very good). The corresponding figure for the non-Ashram villages is 38.00. The difference is statistically significant at 5 per cent level of significance.
- Proportionately more young people in the Ashram seem to prefer taking up agriculture rather than moving out for jobs and the difference is statistically significant.
- In the Ashram area people do not seem to be running after money distributed under various government schemes. They are not keen to avail money under IAY as the money is not found to be sufficient for the kind of houses they want to build as per their natural surroundings—big *khaprail* houses. This shows the lack of contextual thinking on the part of development administration.

When they compare their present condition with the past the residents of the Ashram villages feel happier. To quote Ram Vilas, village Padrach, block Chopan, "We are happy today. The village has salt also. For treatment there are some doctors—good or bad. Earlier we used to cover a distance of 15 km to see a doctor." In general the people living in the Ashram area are happy with the village life and are sceptical about city life. It appears that if they go to city, it is more due to push factors rather than pull factors. Some responses regarding the life in urban areas are: in urban areas people live like insects; urban areas are like *batakia murga* (a duck that is like a chick, scared and coward); for healthy entertainment village is the right place as urban areas are dirty; village people are good by nature; in cities if the power goes everyone will die but in villages somehow life flourishes; there is more air in the villages and more pollution in the cities.

F. Do the youth and elderly people in Ashram villages and other villages differ in terms of measures of well-being?

Ironically, there is more outmigration from the Ashram villages as compared to the Non-Ashram villages (Table 9.5). The differences between the two types of villages are statistically significant.

Table 9.5: Migration from Ashram and Non-Ashram Villages

Items	*Ashram blocks*		*Non-Ashram blocks*		*Total*	
	No.	*%*	*No.*	*%*	*No.*	*%*
N	4509		1212		5721	
Families with at least one member migrating (no.)	1446	32.07	334	27.56	1780	31.11
Families with no member migrating (no.)*	3063	67.93	878	72.44	3941	68.89
Members who migrate (no.)	0.3575	(0.5666)	0.3293	(0.6724)	0.35	(0.591)

* The difference between Ashram and Non-ashram blocks is significant at 5 per cent.

Note: Based on household listing data level of significance.

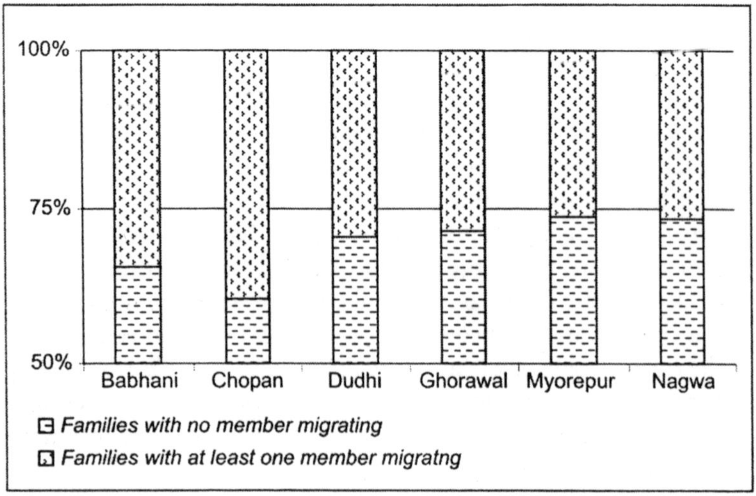

Fig. 9.1: Block-wise situation of migration

Analysis shows that

1. Amongst all the six survey blocks, highest migration is registered in Chopan followed by Babhni block.
2. The migration is largely due to the drought faced by these villages in the last four to five years. The blocks where there are alternative sources of livelihood, such as employment in industries or construction work, migration is somewhat less.
3. Chopan block has the highest rate of outmigration. However, in village Panari of the same block the outmigration is somewhat less. The reason is that there are a large number of check dams and bandhis in the village. Farmers, who are able to irrigate their land, prefer not to migrate out.
4. In Babhni block highest out migration is recorded in Chakbagdari village. The Ashram worker is not very active, less than one-third land is irrigated and more than one-third of the families are in debt. The moneylenders are quite active and they take land as collateral.
5. According to Sarpanch in Ashram and Non-Ashram villages, the migration is on a rise. There are active network of agents who come here employ young people. In Myorepur block the team met an agent who takes hundreds of young people for shuttering work to Chennai, Hyderabad and Bangalore region. Wherever such networks have kicked on, more and more young people are getting pulled into it. Most of them are lured by city life.

Table 9.6: Trend in Migration

Items	*Ashram blocks*		*Non-Ashram blocks*		*Total*	
	No.	*%*	*No.*	*%*	*No.*	*%*
N	30		10		40	
Migration is on rise	24	80.00	7	70.00	31	77.50
Migration is stable	2	6.67	2	20.00	4	10.00
Migration is on decline	4	13.33	1	10.00	5	12.50

Note: Based on Sarpanch data.

Table 9.7: Preference to Stay in Village by Young People

Items	*Ashram blocks*		*Non-Ashram blocks*		*Total*	
	No.	*%*	*No.*	*%*	*No.*	*%*
N	151		50		201	
Prefer to live in village	109	72.19	28	56.00	137	68.16
Prefer to go out of village	39	25.83	15	30.00	54	26.87
Prefer to stay where ever the work is	2	1.32	4	8.00	6	2.99
Cannot say	1	0.66	3	6.00	4	1.99

Note: Based on schedule of young people.

When the young people were asked if they would like to live in their village or would prefer to go out, more youths in the Ashram villages reported a preference to stay in the village (Table 9.7).

However, there is no difference between the advice given by the adults to their children about staying in their own village or migrating out (Table 9.8). In both types of villages majority of people suggest that their children should leave the village. They are more aware of the condition of life in the villages and outside, and they do not seem to visualise a good future in the village, particularly from the perspective of having employment.

Table 9.8: Advice for Young People

Items	*Ashram blocks*		*Non-Ashram blocks*		*Total*	
	No.	*%*	*No.*	*%*	*No.*	*%*
N	603		201		804	
Should go out of the village	394	65.34	137	68.16	531	66.04
Should stay in the village	174	28.86	44	21.89	218	27.11
Cannot say	35	5.80	20	9.95	55	6.84

Note: Based on Schedule of adult people.

Employment outside is connected with education. Respondents in both the Ashram and the non-Ashram blocks have, therefore, developed high aspirations for children's education. Tables 9.9 and 9.10 show the desired level of education for children. Most people want at least High School level education for children. They also feel that boys need to be educated more than daughters. The importance attached to education of sons seems to be higher in the Ashram blocks than in the outside. While they may be happy if their daughters are High School pass they want more education for boys. It also appears that people in the Ashram area are more conservative with respect to daughters' education than non-Ashram blocks. This may be due to the feeling of difficulty in finding a more educated bridegroom, and difficulty in arranging dowry.

Table 9.9: Up to what Level Boys should Study

Items	*Ashram blocks*		*Non-ashram blocks*		*Total*	
	No.	*%*	*No.*	*%*	*No.*	*%*
N	603		201		804	
Up to 5	8	1.33	0	0	8	1.00
6-7	0	0	1	0.50	1	0.12
8-9	18	2.99	7	3.48	25	3.11
10-11	166	27.53	54	26.87	220	27.36
>12	256	42.45	69	34.33	325	40.42
Non-response	155	25.70	70	34.83	225	27.99

Note: Based on Schedule of adult people.

Table 9.10: Up to what Level Girls should Study

Items	*Ashram blocks*		*Non-Ashram blocks*		*Total*	
	No.	*%*	*No.*	*%*	*No.*	*%*
N	603		201		804	
Up to 5	69	11.44	20	9.95	89	11.07
6-7	7	1.16	1	0.50	8	1.00
8-9	60	9.95	25	12.44	85	10.57
10-11	361	59.87	48	23.88	409	50.87
>12	6	1.00	61	30.35	67	8.33
Non-response	100	16.58	44	21.89	144	17.91

Note: Based on Schedule of adult people.

Banwasi Seva Ashram's decades of work in South Sonbhadra has earned the confidence of people. People of older generation fondly recall working with Prem Bhai in constructing check dams, going to night schools and attending meetings at the Ashram. Their faith on Ashram is unfaltering and Ashram is still a beacon they will like to follow. Their expectations from the Ashram are many. People have vociferously asked the Ashram to step in with its educational programmes, both formal and informal. In this water scarce region, it is not surprising that people want the Ashram to take up development work to bring water. There is desperate shortage of water that has affected agriculture and livelihood. Development is synonymous with watershed and irrigation programmes. Some have demanded skill development programmes that will help them improve sources of livelihood. There is also an expectation from the Ashram to provide guidance, wisdom and leadership to the people of the region.

For many of the villagers the connection with the Ashram is lost now. Often in a house, the younger ones and women do not know what all Ashram had done in this region. They do not have any expectations from the Ashram either.

The responses of what young people expect the Ashram to do are shown in Table 9.11.

Table 9.11: Should the Ashram Continue?

Should Ashram increase its activities in the field	*Ashram blocks*	
	No.	*%*
Yes	69	45.70
No	5	3.31
Don't know	56	37.09
Missing	21	13.91
Total	**151**	**100.00**

When asked what specifically the Ashram should do for the young people, the people were not clear. What they could think of is of employment and training. Some could think of educational work and suggested that the Ashram can open more schools in the region (Table 9.12).

G. What are the differences in approaches to sustainability of assets created under the Agrindus project and other programmes between the Ashram villages and the other villages?

There are very significant differences between the implementation

Table 9.12: What Can the Ashram Do?

What could ashram do for young people	*Ashram blocks*	
	No.	*%*
Give employment/training	57	34.55
Open factories so we get employment	4	2.42
Give training (tailoring)	10	6.06
Open school	30	18.18
Watershed development (dig *bawalies*)	3	1.82
Give training for agriculture	4	2.42
Don't know'/can't say	51	30.91
Other	3	1.82
Nothing	3	1.82
Total	**165**	**100.00**

of development programmes in the Ashram villages, under the Agrindus project, and under government schemes. The programmes under the Agrindus project used a holistic and reformist approach rather than the target oriented approach used by thc government. The Ashram also acted reflexively, and based on the experiences of the earlier experiments. For example, in the beginning the Ashram promoted application of modern inputs—seeds, fertilizer and pesticides—to raise agricultural production but gradually and from its own experience the Ashram leaders have come to advocating organic farming. The Ashram works with the people. The lower level functionaries of the government do not think about policies and programmes on their own. They simply implement the decisions of their superiors and lack the power to make changes. This creates a gap between the people and the providers.

H. Are the Ashram villages doing better than other villages in implementation of rural development schemes started by government of India?

Yes. The biggest success story of the Ashram is the story of getting land rights. Through a multifaceted approach employing advocacy, public interest litigation, fieldwork, and mobilization of people it was able to secure land rights of the tribal people. Nevertheless, in other schemes too the Ashram villages have secured a better deal than those outside the Ashram. Conscientization, consciousness, empowerment and social integration have enabled people to get their rights such as timely payment of wages under NREGA, etc.

For a long time the Ashram did not take interest in micro-finance and formation of Self Help Groups (SHGs). The Ashram knew that the main motive of women to form SHGs under different schemes of rural development has not been to involve them in economic activities but to get the revolving fund and distribute it among themselves. Some women volunteers of the Ashram who had their early training in the Ashram have also formed groups. They have proved to be more effective. For example, Phoolwani of Baghdadu (Babhni) is a worker of the Ashram. She set up a successful SHG of 15 women six years back and named it Kasturba Samooh (in the name of Mahatma Gandhi's wife). This group has regular savings, interloaning and strict discipline. Their dependence on moneylenders has gone. The group is active in the village affairs too. The group fought successfully against (a) employment of JCB machine by the contractor in MNREGA, (b) forest officials to stop illegal felling of trees, and (c) contractors' involvement in illegal mining in the area. The group has promoted organic farming in the village and regeneration of forests. The Ashram used SHGs for women empowerment and awareness. Women were encouraged to come together for mutual help and support and for ending their dependence on moneylenders. It is interesting to note that in Naudiha an active SHG which did *arhar* packing was induced to resolve, "We will never sell *arhar*. We shall process it and sell. If someone is desperate for funds she should sell it to SHG only."

The Ashram created awareness about the social audit process for monitoring MNREGA. This was an effective strategy that brought out critical evaluation of scheme, and helped people raise their voice against the system. The Ashram mobilised villagers and Swarajya Sathis informed people about the provision of social audit of MNREGA work. Shubhaji tells that during a meeting the then District Magistrate (DM) told her that social audit would commence soon. The Ashram and its volunteers sent the advanced notices to educate villagers and volunteers about social audit. They informed the people about the concept and explained the process of social audit, and the rights of people. Typically 300 to 500 villagers attended social audit in year 2010. However, over the years people seem to have become less vigilant. During the survey year, social audit was conducted rapidly without any prior information. People in the villages did not even learn about it. According to a facilitator from District Rural Development Authority (DRDA) Sonbhadra: "We had to complete two to four gram panchayats everyday. There was not much time. Average attendance varied from 30 to 60 people."

The sanitation condition in the Ashram villages is relatively better. A walk through the Ashram villages shows courtyards which are well broomed and where garbage is properly disposed. This type of consciousness is missing in the non-Ashram villages. Shobha Bijwar (Nagwa block) talks about the streets that are filthy and where garbage was dumped on both sides of roads.

Overall, the Ashram has created the awareness that if people cooperate with each other and maintain the public property themselves they will be much better off. Only in the Ashram villages one sees that if handpump goes out of order, people themselves fix it. They do not wait for the Sarpanch to arrange for a mechanic. When people in Karamdand village learned that their ground water is fluoride affected, they organized a meeting. It was decided that they will not depend on Sarpanch and will themselves make effort to get filter machine fitted into the handpump. Such efforts are surely more sustainable. On the other hand, in Bijwar village (Nagwa block) the handpump was out of order and no one bothered getting it repaired. Children were seen carrying water on their bicycles from the nearby hamlets.

One surprising element of the survey was that in the Ashram area people are not expecting benefits from the state, what is so prominent in the villages of Uttar Pradesh. No one demanded an IAY house (under Central Government's housing scheme for the rural poor) or recruitment as Shiksha Mitra (education volunteers, who are hired to teach in government schools on a fixed honorarium). This is a significant departure of thought where people are not looking at the state for benefits. Here it is notable that village after village people expressed lack of trust in government officials. They would complain about lack of transparency in the programmes. People do not get to know what is being planned and executed. The problems elsewhere are same but here they realise that when the Ashram did any work, there were more frequent panchayat meetings and discussions on plans and implementation of plans than when government schemes were implemented.

A large number of respondents did not know if they are members of their Gram Sabha. Though a slightly higher percentage of respondents who knew about this in the Ashram villages than the non-Ashram villages. However, the difference was not statistically significant (Table 9.13).

Table 9.13: Membership of Gram Sabha

Membership of Gram Sabha	*Ashram villages*		*Non-Ashram villages*		*Total*	
	No.	*%*	*No.*	*%*	*No.*	*%*
Adult Schedule						
Women	96	31.79	21	21.43	117	29.25
Men	94	31.23	29	28.16	123	30.45
Total	**190**	**31.51**	**50**	**24.88**	**240**	**29.85**
Young Schedule						
Women	15	19.23	2	7.69	17	16.35
Men	19	26.03	7	29.17	26	26.80
Total	**34**	**22.52**	**9**	**18.00**	**43**	**21.39**

Higher level of awareness of their rights has made people more alert and vigilant about the functioning of contractors in the village. Often they raise voice if construction is not done as per the laid out norms. In one village the contractor, engaged for constructing toilets under Total Sanitation Campaign (TSC), was underpaying the labour and was using sub-standard material. People *gheraoed* him and problem was resolved to their satisfaction.

The Ashram's interventions have facilitated state development activities in the area by: (a) making people aware of various government schemes and their rights; (b) by improving participation of people in the meetings of Gram Sabhas; (c) by resisting formation of unrepresentative bodies by the interested civil servants and encouraging decisions in open meetings of the village; and (d) creating ground work for implementation of various schemes such as formation of SHGs.

I. What are the organizational and institutional differences in development planning between the Ashram villages and other villages?

There are no differences in state planning institutions. The development planning in the country is top-down and the development programmes are implemented using the same institutions across the country. In the Ashram villages the institutions created by the Ashram have, however, facilitated effective utilization of government resources. The training provided by the Ashram has also helped the people who subsequently acquired some power position in the state system by fighting panchayat elections.

One of the most important contributions of the Ashram has been in the social sector, particularly in the area of social integration, fighting against social evils, anti-liquor drive, removal of dowry and women empowerment. When the Ashram started functioning, the society of the region, as elsewhere, was characterized by hierarchy, untouchability, and discrimination. People belonging to upper castes did not visit houses of tribals, and tribals did not dine with Scheduled Caste people. Even within the broad caste/tribal groups there was hierarchy. One sub-caste/community would not dine with or touch members of another community. Nobody stood before the Thakurs. In schools children from the Harijan (Scheduled Caste) community were separated from others. The Ashram functionaries remember how in the early days no Scheduled Tribe (ST) volunteer of the Ashram could stay at Jugaul centre. The Ashram promoted the idea of social equality. The Ashram workers would visit all houses, and eat and drink in all houses. When camps were organized on the Ashram premises cooks were drawn from all castes and communities.

The Asharm has definitely left its influence on patriarchal social order. The Ashram opened schools at several places. Teachers were appointed locally and they were oriented to behave like parents and friends. Attempts were made to improve enrolment of girls. These efforts have produced results. People's attitudes towards girls' education changed. Among the role models this produced is a Harijan girl named Manju Madhubala who was educated in the Ashram school, studied upto graduation and has become a famous *virah gayika* (folk singer) of the national level.

J. Does the local administration follow a different approach to development in the Ashram villages and other villages?

No. The local administration does not follow different approaches in the Ashram villages and the non-Ashram villages. The present trend of centralized planning and involvement of voluntary organizations as plan implementing agency is disappointing from the point of view of the Ashram because in this the spirit of voluntary service and community initiative is getting lost. This benefits little and suppresses any voluntary initiative or sacrifice in the interest of the community well-being. Yet, as the several case studies have shown the people of the Ashram are much more conscious of their rights and this provides pressure on the administration to perform better. Yet, there are certain areas in which the Ashram is supplementing the works of the state government. One such area is that of monitoring of pollution and raising environmental consciousness.

9.1 Conclusion

The Banwasi Seva Ashram, and thus the Agrindus project, appeared first time in a situation of famine, ignorance, illiteracy, isolation, lack of irrigation facilities, superstitious beliefs and fatalism, and exploitation by outsider contractors, administrators and moneylenders. Though, as stated by Dr. Ragini Prem, the Banwasis were the people who for some or other political reasons had taken refuge in the forests of this area. After living for long here they evolved their own well developed civilization marked by occupational differentiation, indigenous knowledge systems in diverse areas, and mutual help. Supported by Gandhian ideology, political elite in the country, and money from Indian and international sources the Ashram it had a grand design of developing the forest society in a non-dualistic framework, seeking cooperation from all, the powerful as well as the powerless. The Ashram provided food, knowledge, irrigation facilities, medicine and schools. It linked the tribal villages to the mainstream. The project has succeeded in several areas. Now the socio-economic and cultural milieu stands changed. The old approaches would not work. Isolation is greatly reduced. Westernization is on. Gandhian ideas are losing appeals. Politics has changed. Financial support to the Ashram is dwindling. Banwasi Seva Ashram has a very small endowment fund though some of its activities try to generate working capital. New problems as of environmental pollution have arisen. Villages have schools, development support from government, high aspiration, mobility and new sources of fissures. The Ashram needs fresh blood, financial support as well as fresh ideas.

There is no doubt that the less developed countries like India need low cost models of development. Models of development in which the local people can achieve sustainable levels of development, making them happier and self-supporting. Inspired by Gandhian philosophy and committed to *sarvodaya* and *swaraj*, the Ashram can identify a few villages and make them self-dependent with minimum support from government and outside. These villages will volunteer for self-sustaining growth and refuse the government money for development, which is inadequate, not per their needs, responsible for many feuds and conflicts in the village, and destructive of local resource base. Development experience of such villages, with proper documentation of processes, can be extremely useful for development activists worldwide and even the existing volunteers and functionaries are capable of doing this. However, some support may be sought from outside development experts. The Ashram also has the opportunity to initiate development activities on project basis and along with this provide services and moral support to people although it is very difficult for the Ashram to adopt itself to the new development framework based on impersonal targets, hierarchy, outside control and absence of voluntarism.

One of the new activities that the Ashram can take up is that of capacity building in the area at various levels, i.e. at individual level, institutional level and societal level. At the individual and village levels the Ashram can raise awareness of various government and non-governmental schemes which are implemented in the area and train people in procedures to acquire the benefits. At the Panchayati Raj Institutions level the Ashram can help in motivating people to attend meetings of the Gram Sabhas, learn about new schemes and rules, secure participation in social audit of various schemes, and raise their capacity to meaningfully participate in village development planning. The Ashram can also help in identifying training needs of the elected representatives of the PRIs and government functionaries and develop effective models of training. Lastly, at the societal level, it can link itself with public administration, industry, and business houses to enable them to get feedback on their activities and develop socially and environmentally more responsible approaches. *However, this requires recruitment of professionally trained staff with support from and networking with various national and international agencies. The old volunteers with traditional training and thinking will not be able to do this kind of work.* They need professional training from appropriate agencies. The Ashram has already made a beginning in this.

CHAPTER **10**

Recommendations

This study has produced a number of observations which are useful not only for the evaluation of the Agrindus project or the activities of the Banwasi Seva Ashram but even otherwise for any study of Voluntary Development Organizations (VDOs). We wish to end this study with certain specific recommendations for the future of the Ashram. They are based on statistical inferences, discussion of the WIZMIN experts with functionaries of the Ashram, as well as the expectations of the people (who are the clients of the Ashram activities). There is, however, a caveat here. Recommendations are never based on facts alone and may not be acceptable to the Ashram. They are based on a number of observations: (a) the Ashram has done massive and far-reaching work in the region at a time the tribal population was living a isolated, pathetic life in a pathetic environment; (b) the Ashram could achieve this because of dynamic and effective leadership of Shri Prem Bhai and Dr. Ragini Prem; (c) there was a lot of financial and intellectual support for the Ashram from inside and outside the country; (d) in the recent past resources with the Ashram have been dwindling; and (e) Provincial and Central Governments have taken many development initiatives in the region and the whole context of intervention has changed.

10.1 Development of Model Villages (MVs)

The five decades of work by the Ashram in Sonbhadra, offers an example of an effective and sustainable model of development to the world. Its work on rural development, based on the Gandhian principles has a great appeal to build a non-violent, self-sustaining, egalitarian and yet an open village society. Gandhian principles are especially relevant today when the world is facing serious environmental risks, threatening the very survival of mankind through climate change. As an alternative to government approach, the Ashram has the capacity to develop self-sustaining model for rural development. At the moment, the Ashram is in possession of a very large intervention area of 400 villages while the other resources with the Ashram are too limited to work at this scale. Therefore, it is strongly recommended that the Ashram concentrate its energies on a smaller area. Let us say it focuses on five Model Development Villages (MDV). Later, the model will be available to all villages in the area and others can implement it in a participatory and voluntaristic manner.

This will show right kind of development where *Swaraj* will mean the self-rule and *Sarvodaya* will mean the welfare of all. In other words, these villages will be self- sufficient to make their own plans of development, set their own priorities, implement their own programmes and achieve economic self- reliance. In the proposed model there will be no role of state in development and only a judicious use of mechanisation will be required. The village people will have their own resources and own planning. They will not say no to government interventions but accept only those interventions which are consistent with their own philosophy and planning. Here the agenda will be set by people and not by the outsiders; people and communities will tackle their own problems; man will be in complete harmony with nature and his efforts will nurture and replenish nature. Government policies and programmes, if found inconsistent with their thinking (or which are likely to create disharmony or chaos of any kind) will be rejected. If the Ashram can take up this challenge, such a model could then be replicated at other places in the country.

There may be five other villages where self-reliance and participatory model of development are attempted to benefit from synergy with government schemes, and other five where the Ashram workers are available only as facilitators and consultants. In these villages synergy with other civil society groups may also be explored.

10.2 Institutional Development

The three tier structure created by the Ashram is in place for several decades, and is in need of fresh blood. The old guards of the Ashram would resist change and stick to the old mental maps and philosophies and cultures. The involvement of young people is imperative to energise the system and rejuvenate the developmental activities. Unless the young people make up their mind and work with the rural populace, the dream of a developed Sonbhadra cannot be achieved. The Ashram should make its programmes more youth friendly and induct a young volunteers force into the system.

10.3 Educational Initiatives

The Ashram has participated for a long time in setting up formal and informal educational programmes, initiating educational campaigns, starting movements to increase literacy, and fighting gender bias. It started working at a time when there was no school in the entire region and Sonbhadra district (then part of Mirzapur district) was highly inaccessible. Today the scenario has changed. The rural landscape is cluttered with government and private schools. This study shows that people still need the Ashram to set up schools and to continue with their education policy. Why? The reason is that both the state and the private sector have failed in delivering quality education. People are looking up to the Ashram for giving them literacy, skills, a forum to meet and discuss community issues, and finally, self-esteem and pride. The modern education has only alienated the young people from their villages and their own cultures. As observed by Gandhiji, the modern education has made them look down upon their culture and people, and made them dependent on outside and helpless. The Ashram should intervene.

Some specific activities that the Ashram may take up are as discussed below.

10.3.1 Learning Resource Centre

The Ashram can play a pivotal role in enhancing quality of education by setting up a Learning Resource Centre (LRC) to provide technical support to governmental and non-governmental agencies involved in the field of early, primary and secondary education. It could develop tools and techniques of effective learning, carry out experiments and monitor the programmes. LRC could also assist in bringing out books and producing literature in local language (Hindustani). The LRC should have a basket of items to address the needs in the field of pre-primary, primary and secondary education. The reach of the LRC could go beyond the territories of district Sonbhadra.

Inclusive education is another area that requires serious attention. Inclusive education is a plan of education whereby all sections and social groups are covered. This includes women, tribals, low castes, families of landless labourers, minorities, drop-outs and other vulnerable sections of society. The State of UP and many other States are suffering from shortage of material for people with special needs, for example material in Braille script and resources. There is also a shortage of centres to carry out integrated training of teachers/trainers. The governments do not have the resources required for running programmes for the disabled people. LRC could also provide an important link by developing online libraries, and audio-visual aids. These resources can unfold a new world to the vulnerable and disabled children. Such children can immensely benefit from the Gandhian idea of being productive while learning, rather than merely learning with dependent and precarious support.

While the state is unable to provide sufficient library material to all schools, the LRC should be well equipped with traditional learning resources like books, magazines and audio/visuals as well as electronic information resources on education.

10.3.2 Teachers Training

Government school teachers are in the dire need of teachers' training. Several new concepts, techniques and tools like Teaching and Learning Materials (TLM) have been introduced without proper training of teachers. That is the reason these programmes have not been properly implemented. The District Institutes of Education and Training (DIETs) have the responsibility to train teachers but they lack the capacity and motivation to train thousands of teachers each district has. The Ashram is well positioned to handle training of teachers.

10.3.3 Vocational Training

The Ashram's vocational courses have been of high value and have been very successful. Of late, they seem to have lost the lustre and very few people find them appealing. The reason, as reported by the people, is that the courses offered have not been changed with time but their needs are constantly changing. If three decades back repair of handpumps was the need of the hour, today it is repair of computers and mobile sets. The Ashram has to change with the changing times. Induction of younger trainers may also add vibrancy to the courses. On the other hand tailoring courses for young girls and women have a good demand amongst women even today. They could be strengthened further. There is a need to rethink about the types of skills that are required today, and redesign the courses. These courses may also cater to those who want to establish their own enterprise, in addition to needs of those who are searching for a suitable job in the labour market. A well run vocational training programme will reconnect the youth to the Ashram and its ideology.

In the nutshell, along with setting up its own schools in the Model Villages it should develop LRC and start teachers' training programmes. These programmes would not only respond to the demands of the market they will also promote humanistic thinking, enhance the capacity of teachers at government and private schools, and provide a role model to the teaching community in general. The tools and techniques developed by the team of the Ashram are fairly advanced, and the Ashram's teachers can serve as excellent resource for teachers' training. They could also utilise communication technology to reach out to a larger number of schools.

10.4 Setting up of Agriculture Resource Centre

The Ashram's experience in the land development and agriculture has been fairly long. There is a need to roll out technologies that are suitable for wasteland like that in Sonbhadra district. Indian

Council of Agricultural Research (ICAR) calls for applications from NGOs to set up Kisan Vikas Kendras (KVKs) and meet the technological needs of the farmers. The Ashram is recommended to set up KVK (Krishi Vigyan Kendra) and carry out research in collaboration with prominent institutions of the region, specially the institutes like Allahabad Agriculture University, Naini, and Banaras Hindu University, Varanasi. It can offer such training courses to farmers which are need based and suitable to local conditions and consistent with the Ashram's basic philosophy. In this way the Ashram can achieve two goals: (a) providing a different model of functioning of KVKs; and (b) achieving interaction with specialists and intellectuals in the region which has quite declined in the recent times.

10.5 Promote Organic Farming

Many farmers of Sonbhadra district continued the tradition of organic farming. They knew that it replenishes their land and it is good for their own health. However, due to concern about immediate return and the lure of money, they are compelled to go for modern farming techniques, fertilizers, pesticides and herbicides. They are getting tempted to adopt high yield variety seeds that require increasing use of water, chemical fertilisers and pesticides, and eventually ruin the natural resources. The Ashram can initiate a programme to form cooperative of Organic Growers to promote organic farming. Further, the Ashram could provide the know-how and expertise, help in conducting farm appraisals and seek certification of national and international bodies that will help growers fetch a better price for their product.

10.6 Development of Local Art Forms

Sonbhadra District has various dance forms and arts that could be of interest even outside the district and State. However, on this day one does not meet a local troop or group that is recognised outside the region. The rich culture of the Bundelkhand region is dying. This is something that the Ashram can achieve easily by forming appropriate cultural groups, and linking them to well known cultural groups at the State and Central levels. In the Twenty First Century when cultural and social capital have emerged as two major factors in development, the Ashram can help link the existing cultural groups to national networks, and raise the demand for their cultural pursuits. The Ashram can provide them identity cards to prove their credentials on the pattern of what it has done for the artisans. The goal should be to save the dying art forms of the region.

10.7 Ideological Work/Networking

Last but not the least, the biggest strength of the Ashram is ideological. The Ashram has to develop effective networks/linkages with Voluntary Development Organizations (VDOs) working along similar lines in other parts of the world. The Ashram is best placed to share experiences of development along Gandhian lines. It may link up with Green Movement of Germany and other countries, and attract intellectuals to develop a critical theory of modernization.

In sum, to achieve all the above, to promote the Gandhian vision of *Sarvodaya* and *Swaraj*, and show the path of sustainable development, the Ashram has to follow a more professional approach. Sustainable, self-reliant development is certainly the dream of all those who care about the future of mankind. This has to be nurtured and advanced further. Let all those who read this report also contribute to keeping this dream alive by supporting the Ashram activities in any manner they can.

10.8 Conclusion

Time has come when the Ashram has to look back at its history, analyse its strengths and weaknesses, develop a new understanding of externalities and evolve a new programme keeping in view its financial, social, human and cultural capitals. What worked in the past may not work in the future. What did not work in the past may work now. In the broad framework of *Sarvodaya* and *Swaraj* new strategies have to be evolved. A way has to be found also to attract professional, intellectuals and activists to the Ashram activities in the manners they can find it easy to get involved in. The people of the region trust the Ashram and the Ashram has contributed significantly to promote peace process in the region by countering the discontent leading to Naxalism and both the Ashram and society of India will gain if the Ashram can continue to provide thinking on the peaceful model of universal and inclusive development.

Epilogue

The draft report on the Banwasi Seva Ashram (BSA) was submitted in August 2012. Dr. Ragini Prem, Secretary of the BSA circulated it among some activists, sympathizers and intellectuals. We have received comments from some of them including Dr. Ragini Prem herself. Several of them, which require explanation of figures or are of factual nature, have been incorporated in the report without affecting the objectivity of the report. Yet, there are some perspectival issues. Grassroots action is shaped by ideology, socio-cultural milieu, history of earlier action and many other things. In this epilogue we wish to take up a few important issues raised by two activist thinkers, Mr. Dunu Roy and Mrs. Anna-Maria De Witte. Mr. Roy, M.Tech. from IIT, Bombay is a renowned activist who is assisting urban and rural communities in research and action. His activities focus on shelter, livelihoods, services, and governance. He is also involved in struggle for justice by the urban poor. He is running a Delhi-based research centre, named *Hazards Centre*. Mrs. Anna-Maria De Witte has been associated with the Ashram for a long time and is taking keen interest in the development activities of the Ashram. Originally from Belgium, she is an expert on health and has keenly examined the health component of the Ashram initiatives. I met her in the Ashram in 2006 or 2007 when I had visited the Ashram in connection with a study of youths and found her to be an ardent advocate of voluntarism. The reactions to the report exhibit two different approaches to development initiatives in the country. Since they are perspectival in nature they could not be addressed in the main part of the report. They are included here.

Very much like the WIZMIN team, Dunu Roy recognizes that

the Ashram is not able to resist modernity and is losing the battle to initiatives by the government, liquor barons and industrialization. This is an undisputed fact that state is working against the idea of establishing model self-reliant villages, in isolation from the mainstream economy. Right from the beginning, in independent India the Nehruvian industrial socialism supported federalism and weakened the idea of *Gram Swaraj*. Gandhian ideas are losing their appeal fast, and financial support to the Ashram from both international and national sources is dwindling. However, this is neither a criticism of Gandhian theory nor an argument against continuation of the Ashram activities. While this is true that modernization is proceeding unabated, the adverse consequences of modernization have become more vivid to both socialists and Gandhian activists. And in this context Gandhian theory and existence of the Ashram appear as forceful alternatives. Dunu Roy argues for adopting an agitational approach to deal with environmental crisis caused by the power generation and industrialization in the region. The task is not easy. The Ashram has to educate poor, tribal, those fighting for survival, about causes and consequences of environmental crisis and what is required to solve this crisis in both short-term and long-term. This is going to be a daunting task. When the Ashram fought for them for land rights the villagers saw a concrete personal advantage for them which is not the case with fight against the environmental crisis. People see the environmental crisis as the collective fate and they are not confident of doing anything to mitigate this crisis. They will also not gain individually or collectively in the short run by launching a powerful agitation against the polluters.

Looked at from Dunu Roy's perspectives the Ashram may propose the following programmes. (His suggestions are apt and worth quoting)

(a) Establish through a participatory process in the selected villages what their needs are.
(b) Conduct an analytical exercise to show that the government-sponsored development has not been able to satisfy these needs in the past and is unlikely to do so in the future.

(c) Sharpen this exercise to demonstrate that the government and the industries are able to follow this unsustainable path only because of many *concealed social and environmental costs*.
(d) Map out a resource inventory in the villages and discuss with the villagers how those resources can be used to increase livelihoods and improve access to all services.
(e) Build capacity at all levels to understand that sustainable livelihood is a 'right' and something that the State must provide.
(f) If necessary, take up vocational training and limited demonstrations to illustrate how this "right" is achievable, but not within the limits set by the present model of industrialization.
(g) Build social and organizational pressure through the Gramswarajya Sabhas (GSS) units—similar to the Bhoomi Haqdari Morcha—on the Government to pursue a livelihood-centred development model.
(h) Encourage the youth to take the lead in this campaign so that they can protect their future rights.
(i) At the same time, build capacity among the Ashram personnel to understand the fundamentals of participatory data collection and planning and how to direct these into a campaign around livelihood rights.

The above ideas are, however, broad and there is a need to formulate appropriate proposals for each of them.

Mrs. Anna-Maria De Witte is more critical of methodology, vision of the study team, findings, organization of the report and recommendations. Mrs. Witte is a committed activist and she cannot be happy with anything less than a complete transformation assisted by intellectuals and researchers. This is true that the researchers who participated in the study were professional social science researchers. They were not committed to Gandhian action though some of them can understand and appreciate the Gandhian philosophy of participatory action. But this also helped in the sense that the study team could explore the merits and demerits of various programmes and initiatives launched by the Ashram quite objectively and dispassionately. At no stage the team made any claim to contribute to social movement to be launched by the Ashram or expressed any interest in this. Researchers have their own limits.

Without going into methodological issues like selection of control blocks, which cannot be handled now let us come to the major theoretical points. Mrs. De Witte has certain points which are worth noting. First of all, she notes that in every social domain, there is disinvestment and disinterest on the part of the government. It is almost impossible to find highly placed persons who can see a project through. She claims that monetary schemes, "thrown" at the people like alms, are ineffective—except where the people are well organized mostly (as we say) a small piece of cloth against bleeding. She is doubtful about 'synergies' with the government. This is a viewpoint and we do not need to contradict it. In many evaluation reports of Government schemes we too have expressed the similar frustration with state planning and execution. Secondly, she says that the research has not compared the Ashram's works with other social organizations or social development projects in the region, like those started by Hindalco and other companies, under the Corporate Social Responsibility (CSR). She claims that 'social networking too has become a matter of taking sides with the mighty, shielding one's own "domain", getting people on one's side ....' Though this comparison was not the part of the Terms of References (TOR), based on our earlier experiences we believe that the other social organizations cannot compare with the Ashram in holistic thinking, dedication, vision, and impact. The other organizations are professional, target bound and impersonal. They may benefit by visiting the Ashram to learn effective means of social interventions. Thirdly, Mrs. De Witte is concerned that the Ashram is 'starved of professionally qualified people'. 'The organization does receive plenty of young (and other) visitors, but either they prefer to start their own organization or they fail to rise up to the occasion.' She asks the simple basic life style as of the poor, and the physical as well as social isolation (little food variety, erratic availability of electricity, difficult connections by telephone, mail and road), are too heavy obstacles?' Mrs. De Witte's question is itself the answer to her question. Fourthly, Mrs. De Witte wants that the perpetrators of natural and socio-cultural destruction should be fought against with determination as strongly as during the freedom struggle.

People's organizations in India should learn from Green Parties in Europe in terms of research and support, and from Gandhi and Vinoba for ideology. The problem is that for a variety of reasons Indian people cannot launch the fight against 'the perpetrators of natural and socio-cultural destruction' as they did against the Englishmen. To argue for this is to go into vast literature on environmental movements. As compared to the Englishmen the environmental risks are hidden, subject to interpretations and result of people's desire to change their life. Finally, she wants more comments on what can government and civil society do to promote peace and development, rather than asking the Ashram to 'reformulate strategies'. Although this would form a crucial part of dialogues on development this task was not the part of the study.

On the one hand, Mrs. De Witte is skeptical about the idea of synergy between the Ashram and state, and on the other, she asks why NGOs doing good work cannot be recognized and supported by the government. She gives example of Belgium where 'a great many socially valuable voluntary organizations which flourished in the sixties and seventies, were later recognized by the government and subsidized, as it was acknowledged that they were doing a necessary job falling under the responsibility of the government and that they were of great value for the society (there were meeting centres for youth, advocacy groups for the poor, self-help groups for patients, groups where immigrants and Belgians could meet etc.) The transparency demanded by the government ensured that these organizations either could continue to work properly or in time lost their subsidies and had to stop.' She must realize that India is not Belgium and here NGOs depending on government funds can also be found to be unclean and ineffective either because the founding fathers run them for ulterior motives or the officials granting and distributing funds themselves expect cuts from the funds. No Indian social scientist would ask the question raised by Mrs. De Witte:

> Why cannot the government at least pay wages to now voluntary workers, and in this way help to attract on a long term basis those professionals who are most needed in the rural areas? Why does it not promote more fundamental

> environmental health research by academics *in situ*? It already controls NGOs by demanding proofs of funding and deals out permissions without which they are not allowed to function. Why is it reluctant to give full support where this is badly needed?

It must be recognized that the process of transition from tradition to modernity is not smooth. The movement is multi-lineal and often cyclical. Thus intellectuals have been critiquing the development process from different and often contradictory perspectives. It is natural that the findings of the report on the activities of the Ashram and our recommendations will be looked at from these different perspectives. Overall, there are two major responses to the report. The secretary and dedicated volunteers of the Ashram believe in continuation of the participatory and voluntary works along Gandhian lines. Mrs. De Witte also advocates participation and training of local people to promote livelihood and face the environment crisis, who will in turn train other villagers in the philosophy and strategies of the same. Intellectuals, like Dunu Roy want the Ashram to go into the old struggle mode. To him the method adopted during struggle for land rights should be revoked for environmental movement. This report touches upon the positive impact of the Ashram activities in the region and also on the reasons why the momentum could not be sustained and there is a need to look into the vision and mission afresh. Mrs. De Witte understands this well when she asks: 'Is it not unwarranted to estimate that the power of the Ashram could be such as to make the corporate sector assume all its social responsibilities and promote a shift in the direction of development from growth towards sustainability?' The idea of building model and experimental villages proposed in the report emerges from our reconciliatory approach and the premises that the Ashram has done unparalleled work of development among the poor tribals in the past but it lacks the advantages of the earlier decades. Today not only the character of the state and industrial profile of the region are completely changed, the socio-cultural milieus, resources and networks stand depleted. Moreover, there is no consensus regarding the model of development in India any more. There are more models than the theoretical paradigms. The possibility of saying anything unequivocally is very remote. The report presents a theoretical-pragmatic approach from the Gandhian point of view. And yet, the lamp lit by the Ashram must be protected for the posterity and provide an alternative to those who have a greater skepticism of industrialization and modernization than ever in the past. To follow Mrs. De Witte, we may ask: 'With a growth-obsessed government and political parties tilting towards industries, whom else can the people count on? Either they join the insurrection or they consider the Ashram "as a guardian to us, always there when we need it". This report has not in any way belittled the great and unprecedented work done in the remote tribal areas of Sonbhadra district by the Ashram but is concerned that the financial and social capital with the Ashram is dwindling, and the Gandhian voluntarism is losing to statist model of industrialization and change. It needs new interpretation in different contexts.

References

AFC, 1980, Whole Village Development Programme of AGRINDUS: An Education Report.

Banwasi Seva Ashram, 2003, *Banwasi Seva Ashram: Karya Pragati, March 2003*, Banwasi Seva Ashram, Govindpur, Sonbhadra.

Banwasi Seva Ashram, 2006, *Gram Swaraj Sammelan—7 November*, Banwasi Seva Ashram, Govindpur, Sonbhadra.

Banwasi Seva Ashram, 2006, *Swarn Jayanti Smarika*, Banwasi Seva Ashram, Govindpur, Sonbhadra.

Böckerman, Petri and Ilmakunnas, Pekka, 2006, Elusive effects of unemployment on happiness, *Social Indicators Research*, 79: 159-169.

Dilman, Ilham, 1982, Happiness, *Journal of Medical Ethics*, 8: 199-202.

Fluoride in Drinking Water, State of the Science, Regulatory Update, and Additional Resources, Water Research Foundation (http://www.waterrf.org/Research/ResearchTopics/StateOfTheScienceReports/Fluoride_StateOfTheScience.pdf)

Hoddy, Elizabeth, 1999, *The Banwasi Seva Ashram*, Gandhi Peace Foundation, New Delhi. International Institute of Management, http://www.iim-edu.org/polls/grossnationalhappinesssurvey.htm [accessed on 23 December, 2010].

Jain, L.C., 1996. *Decentralised Planning for Agriculture and Rural Development*, NABARD.

Kelm, Jackie, http://happiness-survey.com/survey/, Appreciative Living LLC [accessed on 23 December, 2010].

Linley, P. Alex, Maltby, John, Wood, Alex M., Osborne, Gabrielle, and Hurling, Robert, 2009, Measuring happiness: The higher order factor structure of subjective and psychological well-being measures, *Personality and Individual Differences*, 47: 878–884.

Martin, Mike W., 2008, Paradoxes of happiness, *Journal of Happiness Studies*, 9: 171-184.

Prem Bhai, 2000, A development agenda for the consideration of voluntary organizations, in *Dhai Akhar Prem Ke*, Banwasi Seva Ashram Govindpur, Sonbhadra.

Ramagundam, Rahul, 2006, *Social Warrior: Nurturing Village based Constructive Workers for Gram Swarajya*, Banwasi Seva Ashram, Mahatma Gandhi Mission.

Roy, Ramashray, and Srivastava, R.K., 1986, *Dialogues on Development: The Individual, Society and Political Order*, Sage Publications, New Delhi.

Ryff, Carol D., 1989, Happiness is everything, or is it? Explorations on the meaning of psychological well-being, *Journal of Personality and Social Psychology*, 57 (6): 1069-1081.

Sharma, A.K., 2008, Developing the rural poor: Experiences of Banwasi Seva Ashram, Sonbhadra, *National Seminar on Revitalization of Rural Institutes: Problems and Prognosis*, Gandhi Smriti & Darshan Samiti, New Delhi, organized by GSP/CSSS/SSS, Jawaharlal Nehru University, 15-16 March, 2008.

Wallin, Pauline, 2008, Three Paths to Happiness, Pennsylvania Psychological Association Convention, June.

Index